CHURCHES IN THE WORLD OF NATIONS

NINAN KOSHY

CHURCHES IN THE WORLD OF NATIONS

International Politics and the Mission and Ministry of the Church

WCC Publications, Geneva

Cover design: Edwin Hassink

ISBN 2-8254-1136-1

Printed in Switzerland

To Susan

Table of Contents

Preface

The idea of writing a book like this one was first suggested to me by some friends in the Commission of the Churches on International Affairs (CCIA) during discussions of the document, "The Role of the World Council of Churches in International Affairs", which was commended to the churches by the WCC central committee in 1985. They felt that it would be useful to explain some of the presuppositions, concepts and insights in greater detail than was allowed by the necessary brevity of that document.

After toying with the idea in different forms, I have tried in these pages to explain in some detail the rationale and theological basis for WCC involvement in international affairs with some illustrations from experience. This book is neither a definitive history of the Commission of the Churches on International Affairs nor a comprehensive and critical study of the WCC's role in international affairs.

The reflections in the book come out of what I have been privileged to learn in my fairly long association with the WCC's work in international affairs. They seek to respond to the many questions that are asked about the "how" and "why" of the WCC's involvement in this area. These are questions not just asked from the outside but also by those who deal with the issues on an almost daily basis.

What I have learned I owe primarily to the many people in those churches around the world which have been in the midst of the critical situations with which the WCC has had to deal. The experiences and insights of persons engaged in costly struggles for human dignity and justice have challenged and enriched me. Often I have felt humbled in their presence. I have also learned a good deal from others with whom my work brought me into contact, including diplomats, political leaders and colleagues in other non-governmental organizations.

I owe the WCC a great debt of gratitude for having allowed me the privilege of serving in one of the key areas of its ministry, an area that has been and continues to be integral to the mission of the church. It was an exciting job during an exciting period in history, which called on the WCC to respond to many critical situations. Although one often felt a sense of personal inadequacy in those circumstances, the resources within the ecumenical movement were encouraging.

Many colleagues in the World Council of Churches have been immensely helpful to me. I shall mention the names of only a few of them, acknowledging the risk of selection and omission: Philip A. Potter, Konrad Raiser, Leopoldo Niilus, who guided me especially in the early period of my work at the WCC; Dwain Epps (who was particularly helpful in the final stages of the book), Erich Weingärtner, Victor Hsu, Christiane Hoeffel and Frans Bouwen, my close collaborators over a long period; Olle Dahlén and Theo van Boven, two moderators of the CCIA during my time on the staff; and Jan Kok and Marlin VanElderen of the WCC Communication Office, who encouraged me to write this book.

NINAN KOSHY

1

Christian Witness and International Affairs

One of the memorable moments during the seventh assembly of the World Council of Churches in Canberra, Australia, in February 1991 came when the general secretaries of the National Council of Churches of Korea (Republic of Korea) and of the Korean Christians Federation (Democratic People's Republic of Korea) appeared together on the podium and embraced each other. Even more significant was the moment in the same assembly when the re-entry into the WCC of the church in China, represented by the China Christian Council, was announced.

For the small Christian community in North Korea, it was the first time to be represented at a WCC assembly. The churches in China, founding members of the WCC, had stopped coming to WCC meetings after 1956 and had not been present at an assembly since the inaugural one in Amsterdam in 1948.

There were no theological or ecclesiological reasons why these two churches were absent for so long from the fellowship of the WCC; and to ensure their presence at Canberra, the WCC had to deal with some critical *political* issues — in Korea, the common quest by the churches in the two parts of the country, encouraged by the WCC, for peace and reunification; and in the case of the church in China, the relation between the People's Republic of China and Taiwan, which required finding a formula enabling the participation in the WCC of both the Presbyterian Church in Taiwan and the China Christian Council. Willingness to confront these difficult political issues was undergirded by the conviction that the unity of the church and the fellowship of the WCC transcend political boundaries.

Most delegates in Canberra were probably unaware that both of these memorable moments at the assembly were preceded by almost a decade of patient negotiations. Fundamental to this process was continuous and careful monitoring of events in the region and in the countries. Making use of the openings for contacts and initiatives followed. The protagonists were not in Geneva, but in the churches and Christian communities concerned. In playing the role of catalyst, the WCC had to grapple with some of the most complex problems in international affairs. It was evident again how important it is for the Council to monitor, analyze and take positions on international affairs in close collaboration with the churches in order to maintain, expand and strengthen the ecumenical fellowship.

But if response to international political issues is integral to the life of the ecumenical movement, this raises several important questions. On the basis of what assumptions does the WCC act in this area? What special considerations and motivations does a Christian organization bring to such action? What are its possibilities and limitations? When should it speak and when should it remain silent? What is its authority? What does it achieve?

The agonizing questions raised by witness in the realm of international affairs are relevant not only for the WCC but also for its member churches. They too act in national and international affairs as part of their ministry — even if sometimes unconsciously. To a large extent, the churches' own experiences and models of actions have shaped and decided the WCC's experiences and models in this field. The prophets, pastors and innovators have been in the churches; and the scope of and constraints on WCC action have often been determined by its member churches.

There are no neat answers to the questions raised, and our treatment of them here will be more in the form of reflections. Rather than describing specific actions, we will seek to look at the "hows" and the "whys" of what the WCC does in international affairs.[1]

As the WCC's name suggests, the whole world is its arena of concern. On the face of it, this claim may appear presumptuous, but it is a fact that any political development taking place anywhere in the world could be of decisive interest and importance to the fellowship of the churches and their mission and ministry. An event which appears insignificant today may be the beginning of something of tremendous significance in the future; conversely, a dramatic event of the present probably has its roots in events unnoticed some time ago. A trend that begins in one part of the world may later become common in many places. A decision taken in one capital may alter the course of history in many other countries. It may be too much to claim that the WCC is able to monitor carefully all events in every part of the world, but there is a constant demand on the Council to be familiar with developments especially as they affect the life and witness of the churches.

In the fellowship of the WCC there are more than 320 member churches, in nearly 100 countries, North, South, East and West, in different socio-political systems and in a variety of historical and cultural settings. Any national or international political development can affect this fellowship; and strains and strengths can be noticed only by carefully monitoring events in the situations where the churches are called upon to witness.

Certain tensions inherent in the WCC are generally creative but have some special implications in dealing with international affairs. Constitutionally, the Council is a *fellowship of churches* that "confess the Lord Jesus Christ as God and Saviour according to the scriptures", to whom the WCC "shall offer counsel and provide opportunity for united action". Thus the particular needs, possibilities and problems of each of its members must always be taken into account. But the WCC, in its self-understanding, is also a *frontier movement* which must be ahead of the churches, providing new responses to challenges and taking new initiatives. At the same time, the WCC is a large *international organization*, with a very broad constituency, making it a not-insignificant actor on the world scene. It is not easy for the WCC to function on these three different levels at the same time. Each has its own style, methods of action and expectations. This may create tension and sometimes apparent inconsistencies in the formulation of WCC positions on international affairs.

At the level of expressing the fellowship of churches, the emphasis naturally falls on achieving maximum consensus. This should not, however, lead to the temptation of seeking the lowest common denominator. In any given situation, being overly sensitive to the special position of an individual member church may result in inaction and apparent support of an unjust status quo. Moreover, action at the international level usually has a direct effect on the life and witness of several churches. So an attempt must be made to accompany the church in its ministry, raise critical questions, create broad consensus and then move forward.

If this moving forward is not possible, the character of the WCC as a frontier movement will be lost. The WCC should be ready to take risks. If it hesitates to confront a member church on critical issues it may not be able to fulfil its vocation. At the same time, if it is too far ahead of the churches, it will be unable to move them along with it as it displays its character as a frontier movement and takes bold steps for the unity of the churches and the unity of humankind.

As an international organization the WCC's actions and styles of functioning are often compared with those of other international organizations working for justice, peace and human rights — sometimes in the form of critical questions: "Amnesty International has said this; why has the WCC said nothing?" "Why is the WCC acting in this way when the International Commission of Jurists has drawn a different conclusion?" Such questions do not come up only within the churches; increasingly, expectations and assessments of the WCC's actions in international affairs come from secular bodies, diplomats and other international organizations.

In 1985 the WCC central committee commended to the churches a document on "The Role of the World Council of Churches in International Affairs", which explains the rationale and theological basis of this involvement, sets forth procedures and forms of action and draws out the implications of these for the fellowship and unity of the churches. Based on affirmations, findings and insights from various parts of the Council, the document underlines the link between work in international affairs and work connected with mission and unity. The foreword observes that "activities in the realm of political affairs are expressed through all parts of the ecumenical movement, both because of the nature and reach of politics and because of the Council's holistic understanding of the mission of the church."[2]

We begin in Chapter 2 with a bit of history to show the importance of concern for international affairs, especially for peace, in the growth of the ecumenical movement. The fact that the church is international and ecumenical was expressed in the formation of an instrument called the World Council of Churches. Concern for international affairs was integral to the WCC from its very beginning, and so it is natural to start with a look at our heritage.

From the outset leaders of churches maintained that ethical norms and behaviour are important in the international realm and that international law should have a moral basis. It has always been recognized that the churches should develop resources to translate their convictions about participation in international affairs. This discussion of ethics and international affairs (Chapter 3) continues to be highly relevant today.

Nevertheless, it is sometimes alleged that the churches do not really have the competence to deal with the complexities of international affairs.

They are accused of "zeal without knowledge". So we go on to consider in Chapter 4 what resources are available to a body like the World Council of Churches.

It is often the egoism of nations, combined with varying degrees of self-righteousness and perceptions of national interests, that complicates international relations. In Chapter 5 we ask where the church stands in all this. How do church, nationalism and the international fellowship interact? At a time when the nation-state and nationalism are in flux, it is necessary to look afresh at the question of church-state relations.

WCC action in the realm of international affairs is often equated with its public speaking. In fact, this is only one form of action, and other methodologies and styles are more suitable for certain issues and situations. Diplomacy has to do with behaviour and strategy in international affairs. Over the years the WCC has developed its own form of non-governmental diplomacy, and in Chapter 6 we take a look at this.

Nevertheless, public statements may be genuinely important, though several legitimate questions are raised with regard to them. The important questions about criteria for speaking out, selection of issues, who speaks for the church and the authority of the WCC's pronouncements are treated in Chapter 7.

Are actions by a body like the WCC in international affairs effective? Chapter 8, "A Politics of Hope", looks into this question, recognizing that there are differences in perceptions of success and in assessment of results.

The beginnings of the WCC coincided with the outbreak of the cold war, which proved decisive in international relations for more than 40 years. Today there is a new global situation. A preliminary look (Chapter 9) at emerging global trends in the post-cold war period may help in identifying the churches' new challenges and tasks in international affairs at the close of the twentieth century.

NOTES

[1] For a useful brief history of the Commission of the Churches on International Affairs (CCIA), which has been the main organ of the WCC in this field, see Ans J. van der Bent, *Christian Response in a World of Crisis*, Geneva, WCC, 1986.

[2] "The Role of the World Council of Churches in International Affairs", Geneva, WCC, 1986, p.3.

2

The Heritage

The World Council of Churches was founded just after the second world war ended. This period marked the beginning of the cold war — "an armed truce precarious and dangerous"[1] which would continue for more than forty years and operate as the defining reality of international life through the first four decades of the WCC.

Even before the WCC was formally constituted, however, it had to deal with human rights violations and refugee problems while attempting to nurture the new fellowship and to build bridges linking the churches and nations divided by war. The reverberations of the global war were far from over at the time of the WCC's inaugural assembly in Amsterdam in 1948. New international tensions were mounting. Millions of European refugees from the war had still to be resettled, while a new mass exodus was beginning in Palestine. The nuclear arms race had begun. There was a new revolutionary ferment in what was then called the under-developed region; and the yearning for independence of many countries appeared to be threatening the colonial world order.

The renowned Czech theologian Josef Hromádka spoke to the Amsterdam assembly of the responsibility of the church in "abnormal times":

> The church of Christ has to deal with the basic issues of our present international life both with extreme caution and courageous clarity. We are living... on volcanic ground pregnant with destructive explosions and earthquakes. The old international order is gone. No great issue has been solved, not one area of our earth has achieved stability and security... never in the past has the whole of the world been shaken so profoundly as during the last thirty years. Since the last war the magnitude of the international crisis has manifested itself with such inescapable pressure that every thoughtful person feels the proximity of an avalanche which at the mere echo of a loud voice may bury what has been left of our civilization and spiritual heritage.[2]

Even so, it was widely believed that the churches faced this situation with a great new asset: the ecumenical movement. "As though in preparation for such a time as this," said Archbishop of Canterbury William Temple, "God has been building up a Christian fellowship which now extends into almost every nation and binds citizens of them all together in unity and mutual love... It is the great new fact of our time."[3]

New as it was, this fellowship already had a record of confronting international affairs, especially the issues of war and peace. In 1907, forty years prior to Amsterdam, some visionary Christian leaders had made an intervention at the Second Hague Peace Conference on the basis of what they felt was the duty of Christians and churches. Writes one commentator:

> Without theory, without theology, they asked the Second Hague Peace Conference to take certain actions. General though their requests were, they were specific enough to go beyond the stating of general principles. Since that time the ecumenical organizations have taken actions for which there was no "chapter and verse" cited; they simply acted pragmatically when faced with a new challenge.[4]

True, "chapter and verse" were not cited, but it is not correct to say that there has been no theory or theology.

A growing fellowship

By the time the first world war broke out in 1914, the conviction was growing that international cooperation among Christians is part of the mission of the church. Threats to world peace had inspired direct attempts to unite Christians in service to the cause of peace, not leaving this to political leaders alone. Churches and their leaders were seen as responsible for applying Christian principles and insights to international relations and promoting mutual understanding between nations for the development and strengthening of international law. This sense of responsibility undergirded the strong memorandum presented to the Second Hague Conference in 1907, which expressed the Christian conviction that arbitration should be the means for settling conflicts between the nations.

A pioneer in modern ecumenical efforts to solve international problems was the World Alliance for Promoting International Friendship through the Churches. To be sure, the outbreak of the first world war immediately after this international association for peace was founded presented serious obstacles to Christian cooperation in international affairs. As Nils Ehrenström wrote, "the war made communications between the various Christian countries difficult if not impossible... The growing unity of Christendom was rent asunder. Yet fellowship was not wholly destroyed. Some points of contact still remained."[5] A peace appeal issued in November 1914 at the initiative of Church of Sweden Archbishop Nathan Söderblom was, as he himself declared later, "the beginning of more than we surmised at that time..., the starting point of what later developed into the Life and Work movement" — a fellowship of Christians that transcended national boundaries.

An epoch-making event in international cooperation of churches took place in Stockholm in 1925. The Universal Christian Conference on Life and Work affirmed the churches' obligation to apply the gospel in all realms of human life — industrial, social, political and international. The idea of the church as a *transconfessional* reality had always been part of ecumenical thinking. By establishing contacts between Christians who had been on different sides in the war, the Life and Work conference underlined the affirmation that the church universal is also a *supra-national* reality.

This supra-national character was emphasized in a joint declaration of Life and Work and the World Alliance in 1926, calling on all churches to do everything in their power to cultivate international fellowship on a Christian basis. In Ehrenström's words,

> It was a bold affirmation of faith, a banner held higher and higher with unflinching fortitude as the international barometer set towards "stormy" in the 1930s. The tested experience of a wider Christian fellowship transcending barriers of nation and race, the coincident growth of international confessional organizations, the advance of theological thought about the nature of the church and paradoxically the adverse influence of resurgent nationalism — all these combined to bring this article of ecumenical faith increasingly to the fore.[6]

How does this fellowship, professed as an object of faith and experienced as a fact, bear on the shaping of international relations? Ehrenström himself answers the question:

> As the Body of Christ embracing people of all nations and kindreds and peoples and tongues, the universal church is committed to serve as an exemplar, a pattern and a leaven of true world community. By its very existence and in the measure that it realizes its own unity it is the strongest potential factor for international and inter-racial peace.[7]

The hopes, the expectations and the claims were high, perhaps too high. Wilfred Monod called on the worldwide church to give a "soul" to the League of Nations. Max Huber, former president of the World Court and of the International Committee of the Red Cross, argued that a "supranational ethos" must be the source of international law and that "only Christians as members of the Una Sancta understand the deep foundations of a legal order which can extend beyond the limits of the national communities. Only on the basis of the Una Sancta can a supranational ethos be built up."[8]

> To a large extent the task of formulating common Christian convictions concerning the difficult worldwide social and international problems came to be entrusted to the organs of the ecumenical movement. At the end of the second world war there was a strong feeling that a new ecumenical instrument was needed if the churches were to play an effective role in international affairs. Thus the Commission of the Churches on International Affairs (CCIA) was established at a conference of church leaders in Cambridge, England, in 1946, jointly sponsored by the International Missionary Council and the World Council of Churches, then still in the process of formation. While this particular structure had no precedent, the converging ecumenical movement had been building a solid foundation for it over a period of some thirty years.

At a CCIA symposium in 1948, historian Arnold Toynbee said that

> Christianity of course has a role in all human affairs, because Christianity is concerned with the relation of human souls to God, and all human affairs are part of God's creation and God's kingdom. Politics in general and international affairs in particular are the slum areas of human life, in which human beings have been much less successful than, for example, in family affairs or technological affairs.[9]

Whether human beings have in fact been successful in family affairs or technological affairs may be debated, but Toynbee's emphasis on Christian responsibility in the "slum areas" of life remains pertinent.

O. Frederick Nolde, the first director of CCIA, maintained that the basic contribution of Christians to living together in a divided world grows out of "their common faith, their worldwide fellowship and the recognition that the will of God is relevant to the whole family of men upon earth".[10] But he believed that generalities do not suffice. Christians must be concrete about the manner in which God's will should be heeded for the promotion of peace and justice.

This conviction led during the 1950s to specific positions and actions by the International Missionary Council and the WCC, which proclaimed that God's will relates to human affairs and that concern for international affairs is integral to the mission of the church.

By 1967, after twenty years, CCIA felt the need to take a new look at the role of the ecumenical movement in international affairs and the instruments for this involvement. This was a period of revolutionary aspirations, especially in the newly independent and developing countries; and a consultation in The Hague on the future of the CCIA thus took place at a time of profound shifts in international politics.

While marking significant changes in the WCC's dealing with international affairs, the consultation reiterated and clarified the theological presuppositions of the Council's work in this area.

> The biblical message of God's love for all men and his taking upon himself of human nature and history in Jesus Christ impels the churches to be of service to mankind in every aspect of life including international relations. We are all agreed that this service and witness is an essential part of the church's mission.[11]

The report of the consultation listed several theological accents, including the oneness of all humanity under the law of God, "the dynamic element in human history moving to a glorious consummation" and the inspiration to action and the challenge it presents to an imperfect and sinful world. "Starting from the church's participation in the continuing threefold ministry of Christ in the world, the emphasis falls on priestly intercession, prophetic judgement, the arousing of hope and conscience and the pastoral care for mankind."[12] This in essence is the mandate of the World Council in international affairs.

Linking the unity of the church and the unity of humankind, the report spoke of the special perspective on the world that the unity of the church provides:

> The discovery of their unity transcending without destroying the ecclesiastical tradition and national loyalties of Christians throughout the world gives Christians a new perspective from which they may come to more objective judgement of the conflicts of our time.[13]

WCC assemblies speak

At a broader level, WCC assemblies have regularly emphasized the Council's role and responsibility in international affairs.

The first assembly in 1948 recognized that the establishment of the WCC could be an important event in international affairs, since the Council is "a living expression" of a fellowship that transcends

> race and nation, class and culture, knit together in faith, service and understanding. Its aim will be to hasten international reconciliation through its own members and through the co-operation of all Christian churches and of all men of goodwill... It should not weary in the effort to state the Christian

> understanding of the will of God and to promote its application to national and international policy.[14]

The second assembly (Evanston 1954), insisting that "this troubled world, disfigured and distorted as it is, is still God's world",[15] emphasized that reconciliation is necessary for an international order conformed to the will of God. Belief in the gospel of reconciliation makes Christians reject the idea that war is inevitable: "war is not inevitable because God wills peace".[16]

Members of the church must rise above the limits of nationalism and "carry into the turmoil of international relations the real possibility of the reconciliation of all races, nationalities and classes in the love of Christ".[17] The international sphere is a field of obedience to Jesus Christ. It does not fall outside the range of his sovereignty or the scope of the moral law.

The third assembly (New Delhi 1961) reaffirmed the "incalculable value" of the very existence of the ecumenical movement, describing the visible unity of the church as a service to world peace. New Delhi also gave some very helpful guidelines for fellowship and solidarity, saying that the churches must hold each other in brotherly concern and prayers, sustain each other in witness under all circumstances and affirm their fellowship with Christians of all races and nationalities through worship, suffering, joy and service in the unity of the Spirit.[18]

Again emphasizing the unity of humankind, the fourth assembly (Uppsala 1968) added a new perspective which had a major influence on subsequent WCC programmes and policies: "The Word of God testifies that Christ takes the side of the poor and the oppressed."[19] As God makes all things new, Christians are called to critical examination and unhesitating involvement in social and political life at a time of accelerating change. Uppsala also underlined God's reconciling work in ending all division and enmity and recognized new and greater possibilities for concerted action by churches in international affairs. At the same time, it called for a more active and visible role for the WCC, a call which was taken seriously as the Council moved into action-oriented programmes in many areas, including international affairs.

The fourth assembly also urged that the churches broaden their resources for international involvement through dialogue with people of other faiths and all people of goodwill.

There was no special section on international affairs at the fifth assembly (Nairobi 1975). In its section on "Structures of Injustice and Struggles for Liberation", the assembly did say that "in seeking its particular place in today's struggle for social justice and human liberation, the church needs to be constantly guided by its divine mandate".[20]

The sixth assembly (Vancouver 1983) recognized that on critical issues in international affairs churches take different starting points and different approaches, "due to the wide diversity of our histories, traditions and the contexts in which we live and witness". Vancouver urged the churches to:

a) intensify their efforts to develop a common witness in a divided world, confronting with renewed vigour the threats to peace and survival and engaging in struggles for justice and human dignity;
b) become a living witness to peace and justice through prayer, worship and concrete involvement;
c) take steps towards unity through providing more frequent opportunities for sharing in and among the churches in order to learn more about and understand better each other's perspectives, defying every attempt to divide or separate us; and
d) develop more innovative approaches to programmes of education for peace and justice.[21]

The political imperative

We have tried in this brief historical survey to show that dealing with political issues has always been part of the tradition of the ecumenical movement, out of the conviction that concern for politics is integral to the mission of the church. The imperative for Christian participation in politics has been stated succinctly by Ronald H. Preston:

> Politics is an inescapable reality. It is no service therefore to denigrate politics, nor on the other hand to be starry-eyed about it. Christians are liable to become nervous at this point and to wish to be non-political. This is not possible. To be non-political in the sense of doing nothing is tacitly to support things as they are, and to do so irresponsibly without thinking about it.[22]

The World Conference on Church and Society (Geneva 1966) clearly underlined the need for Christian participation in politics:

> Christians have been called by God to fulfil a mission in the world, and obedience to this call means full participation in the life of the world. They have responsibility as citizens, and no concentration on man's eternal destiny can be used as a means to evade the responsibility for his welfare now.[23]

While rejecting any understanding of Christian life as "aloofness" from the world or of political life as an inappropriate sphere for the Christian presence, the Geneva conference also pointed to the "deep ethical ambiguities" and "strong tensions" which may emerge for individual Christians and within the Christian community as a result of this involvement.

> Each concrete situation and each specific position to be taken involves the making of decisions in which there are often sharp conflicts of values and loyalties or in which the issues are blurred and almost indistinguishable. Full recognition of these ethical dilemmas is important both for the Christian and the church. There is no clear set of universally valid rules which provide an immediate answer to these dilemmas nor can the solution be found through a simple application of abstract principles to concrete situations.[24]

In becoming politically involved, Christians should recognize that no political project can ever be presented as absolute and sacred. No temporal society, present or future, can claim full identity with the kingdom of God. The best it can hope for is to carry out some aspects of its role that will foreshadow the perfection of God's kingdom.

It is thus the duty of the church, says André Bieler, "to perceive and announce the signs of this kingdom. And it is also its duty to denounce any attempt at presenting a political project, whatever it may be, as absolute and sacred."[25] The church must always emphasize the necessary and useful nature of politics while pointing out its temporal and relative character.

Politics has to be regularly reconsidered and re-evaluated according to the measure of Christ and his kingdom. And this judgement itself must constantly be revised in terms of changing circumstances and according to the new historical and scientific data that bear on each situation.

This tentativeness does not diminish the significance of political choice. Politics is decisive in the lives of people, and it is one realm in which a Christian can visibly express faith. It is an important vocation for the individual Christian, for the churches and the ecumenical movement. Obedience to the gospel demands such an expression of faith.

As Bieler points out, "there is always an unavoidable risk in action, a risk inherent in the very nature of the commitment of Christian faith. Obedience always includes for the Christian a risk but a risk taken in full confidence of God's love and pardon."[26]

Recalling the context of the second world war, Philippe Maury underscores just how risky political action can be:

> Political blunders will make us responsible before God for injustice and suffering. Our good political intentions may well become the paving stones of hell. But Christian life is lived by faith, not sight, and is always made up of these risks.[27]

Yet, adds Maury, there is a theological perspective that bears on the running of such risks:

> It is God himself who requires us to run these risks, and this is the only reason we are able to assume them. For the Lord who commands us is also the Saviour who forgives. For we cannot bear on our shoulders the burden of history, but thanks be to God, he has already taken it upon himself.[28]

As Donald E. Messer observes, "the prospect of 'dirty hands' and the prescription to weigh risks reinforce the need to articulate a methodological 'tool' that can be used for analyzing conflicting policy recommendations and directions. Such an instrument might enable the conscientious Christian to think and act more responsibly amidst ambiguous and complex social questions."[29]

We shall look more closely in the next chapter at the question of how moral and ethical considerations relate to the involvement of Christians and churches in international affairs.

NOTES

1 Daniel Yergin, *Shattered Peace*, Middlesex, Penguin Books, 1977, p.6.
2 Hromádka, in *The Church and the International Disorder*, London, SCM Press, 1948, p.114.
3 Cf. A.C. Craig and Hugh Martin, eds, *Christian Witness in the Post-War World*, London, SCM Press, 1946, p.21.
4 Darril Hudson, *The Ecumenical Movement in World Affairs*, London, Weidenfield and Nicholson, 1969, p.154.
5 In *A History of the Ecumenical Movement*, Vol. I, eds Ruth Rouse and Stephen Charles Neill, Geneva, WCC, 1993, p.516.
6 *Ibid.*, p.577.
7 *Ibid.*, p.578.
8 *Ibid.*
9 Arnold J. Toynbee, in *Christian Responsibility in World Affairs*, London, CCIA, 1949, p.5.
10 Frederick Nolde, *The Contribution of the WCC to Living Together in a Divided World*, Geneva, WCC, 1955. p.3.
11 Report of the Consultation on the Church in International Affairs, The Hague, April 1967.
12 *Ibid.*
13 *Ibid.*
14 *The First Assembly of the World Council of Churches*, London, SCM Press, 1949, pp.94-95.
15 *The Evanston Report*, Geneva, WCC, 1954, p.131.
16 *Ibid.*, p.134.

[17] *Ibid.*, p.142.
[18] *The New Delhi Report*, Geneva, WCC, 1961, p.109.
[19] *The Uppsala Report*, Geneva, WCC, 1968, p.61.
[20] *Breaking Barriers: Nairobi 1975*, ed. David M. Paton, Geneva, WCC, 1976, p.100.
[21] *Gathered for Life — Official Report of the Sixth Assembly*, ed. David Gill, Geneva, WCC, 1983, p.137.
[22] Ronald H. Preston, *Church and Society in the Late Twentieth Century*, London, SCM Press, 1983, p.115.
[23] *World Conference on Church and Society, Official Report*, Geneva, WCC, 1967, p.110.
[24] *Ibid.*
[25] André Bieler, *The Politics of Hope*, Grand Rapids, Eerdmans, 1974, p.113.
[26] *Ibid.*, p.114.
[27] Philippe Maury, *Politics and Evangelism*, New York, Doubleday, 1959, p.95.
[28] *Ibid.*, pp.95-96.
[29] Donald E. Messer, *Christian Ethics and Political Action*, Valley Forge, Judson Press, 1984, p.109.

3

Ethics and International Affairs

During the Pelopponesian war in the 4th century BC, Athens attacked the small island of Milos. The Melians tried to negotiate the conflict by arguing a moral case against the Athenian intervention: "We are standing for what is right against what is wrong... We invite you to allow us to be friends of yours and to make a treaty which shall be agreeable to both you and us, and so to leave our country." The Athenians replied that in international affairs the strong do what they can and the weak do what they must. Any discussion of rights is valid only among equals. While the Melians insisted on talking about rights and justice, the Athenians conquered and killed them. The twenty-four centuries since this episode have been replete with instances that seem to confirm the view of the Athenians that there is and indeed can be no morality in international affairs.

Morality in international affairs

Not that the language of morality and ethics with regard to the affairs of nations is used only by religious leaders. Appeals to ethics are heard often in the discourse that goes on in the halls of the United Nations and in other international forums. Explaining his own country's concern about human rights in other countries, a senior official of a Western government claimed at a UN meeting not long ago, "Yes, we are our brothers' keepers".

Some political leaders go even further in using moralistic rhetoric and theological categories to defend their foreign policies. The Gulf War of 1991 provides a striking example: for US President George Bush it was a "just war"; for Iraqi President Saddam Hussein, the war against the United States was a *jihad*, a holy war.

Unfortunately, the history of international relations is to an alarming degree a history of selfishness and cruelty. So, despite the rhetoric, the question whether moral standards in fact apply to international affairs is often raised. The veteran US diplomat George Kennan once remarked that the conduct of nations is "not fit for moral judgement" — an ambiguous remark which elicited the observation from one commentator that it seemed to betray a nostalgia for moral assessment while announcing scepticism about its very possibility.

Three broad views on morality and international affairs may be identified. One holds that moral categories and judgements are simply out of place in this realm. On this view, in the field of international affairs, lies are not lies and murders are not murders. Although few political leaders will explicitly say this, many in fact act according to it. A second view, which claims to be "realistic", argues that international relations are conditioned by power and that the conduct of nations is and should be guided and judged exclusively by the requirements of national interests. There are serious difficulties about defining national interests and judging what the requirements for them are. Third, there are those who insist that international relations are subject to moral requirements and ethical criteria, and that only if such requirements and criteria are accepted can we have any hope of even a minimum of peace and justice in the world.

Reinhold Niebuhr was among those who have maintained that questions of right and wrong are inevitably raised in international affairs. According to Niebuhr, "the moral issue in international relations is in fact a more vivid explication of the moral question in the whole realm of political order".[1]

Paul Ramsey quotes what he calls a "remarkable and markedly misunderstood address" on "Ethics in International Relations Today" delivered in 1964 by Dean Acheson, former US Secretary of State. While arguing that "in foreign affairs only the end can justify the means", Acheson immediately went on to say, "This is not to say that the end justifies any means or that some ends can justify anything."[2] Acheson's address attacked the discussion of ethics in connection with politics as a prolific cause of confusion. What passes for ethical standards for government policies in foreign affairs, he said, is a collection of moralisms, maxims and slogans which neither help nor guide but only confuse decision-making.

Stanley Hoffman poses the moral problem in international affairs in a different way. He identifies two central questions: Is there a possibility of moral choice for statesmen in international relations? And, secondly, if one assumes there is, what are the limits of moral choice?[3]

To the first question most people would probably say there *should* be a choice, but many believe and maintain that in fact there *can* be none. Nations exist in a state of anarchy, conflicts, desires and scarcity, which creates a general struggle for power. In this competition the only universal concern is survival. Even those who would like to pursue loftier goals cannot escape from the contest forced by those who are greedy for power. In such a situation, there is no morality. International relations is the domain of necessity, in which the only ends dictated by the nature of the game are security and survival, on behalf of which any means can be used.

Hoffman does not accept such a stark description of international politics as a state of war. "Not at all times are states in a situation of war of all against all; it is not true throughout history; it is not true in space at any one point."[4] Arguing that there is a moral choice for statesmen, Hoffman then turns to the limits of such choice.

The first is structural: the international milieu simply does not leave much room for moral choice.

> A statesman in the international competition cannot afford moral behaviour so easily; first, because of what might be called the state's duty of selfishness. Secondly, in international relations, by contrast with domestic politics, the scope of moral conflicts is infinite, whereas in a domestic order the scope is normally much more restricted. Thirdly, violence, the ever-present possibility of war, limits the range of moral opportunity. There is the state's security dilemma: the need to survive.[5]

The second limit is a philosophical one: there is in fact no single operational international code of behaviour. Rather, there are competing codes, rival philosophical traditions, clashing conceptions of morality. The only common code is not ethics but national egoism. Even if "all statesmen use the same moral language" of "rights and wrongs, justice and law..., from the point of view of moral harmony this is meaningless. A community of vocabulary is not the same thing as a community of values".[6]

Hoffman also points to a political limit on moral choice:

> The statesman's ethics cannot ever be a perfect ethics of responsibility because he does not control what goes on outside and because he normally does not even understand clearly what goes on inside. The difficulty of assessment is created by the fact that events are always ambiguous.[7]

Domestic pressures may also severely restrict the statesman's range of action abroad. Foreign policy decisions may influence the opinion of the voters, and politicians do not want to lose electoral support due to adverse reactions at home to foreign policy actions.

What kind of ethics?

Having referred to the "ethics of responsibility", we should mention here the classification made by Max Weber in a famous essay entitled "Politics as a Vocation". Weber distinguishes "an ethic of ultimate ends" and "an ethic of responsibility". Those statesmen guided by the former, he argues, are more concerned about "the flame of good intentions" than about the consequences of their choices, with which they and their nations will have to live. He contrasts the two types of ethics by saying that the Christian who follows the ethic of ultimate ends "does rightly and leaves the results to the Lord... Conduct that follows the maxim of an ethic of responsibility has to give account of the foreseeable results of one's action."[8]

Commenting on this, John C. Bennett and Harvey Seifert say that "the ethic of responsibility that involves concern for foreseeable results is usually the right approach in public issues which affect the lives and well-being of nations".[9]

Weber himself admits that under certain circumstances an ethic of ultimate ends and an ethic of responsibility may supplement each other: when a mature person "is aware of a responsibility for the consequence of his conduct and really feels such responsibility with heart and soul. He then acts by following an ethic of responsibility, and somewhere he reaches the point where he says: 'Here I stand, I can do no other.'"[10] In the words of Archbishop John Habgood, "any moral approach to politics must somehow weave together" an ethic of responsibility and an ethic of ultimate ends.[11]

Hoffman believes that the ethics of a statesman is and must be an ethics of responsibility, "in the sense of being concerned for the foreseeable future". Even a prophet like Ayatollah Khomeini, a revolutionary like Lenin or a saint like Gandhi must be concerned with consequences, both because they are responsible to their own people and because neglecting consequences might have unfavourable results for their own creed.[12]

He goes on to offer some valuable comments on the relation between means and ends, using an example from the Middle East.

> The goal of Israeli security is certainly a good one, but not if it has to be achieved by creating massive insecurity for the Arabs and particularly for the Palestinians. Justice for the Palestinians is a rightful end, but not if it entails

> indiscriminate terror against innocent Israelis. In other words, international relations is an endless chain of ends and means. Today's means shape tomorrow's ends. It is morally necessary to choose means which are not destructive of one's end through coercion or corruption; secondly, the means must be proportional both to the end, and to the importance of the end in the hierarchy of one's goals, and finally, one ought to choose means which do not entail costs of values greater than the cost of not using these means.[13]

However, the calculation of effects in international affairs is a complex affair, and it is often difficult to decide whether particular means will achieve the intended results. Thus, says Hoffman,

> even an ethics of consequences needs to be saved from the perils of unpredictability and from the temptations of Machiavellianism by a corset of firm principles guiding the choice of ends and means — by a dose of ethics of conviction covering both goals and instruments.[14]

This entails another important way in which morality should influence policy, which Hoffman calls a "morality of self-restraint": a nation's acceptance of moral limits on the means it will use and its recognition that other nations have moral claims as well.

Bennett and Seifert add two other areas in which morality should enter into the formation of foreign policy and the relations between nations. It should determine the fundamental motives and attitude of citizens and policy-makers. "Concern for people as people everywhere, involving both respect and compassion, should always be present."[15] And morality should influence the criteria by which immediate and long-term objectives are determined. "These objectives should be favourable to what we see as the universal good, but they should not be tied absolutely to the ideological slant from which we interpret that universal good."[16]

Morals and moralism

Bennett draws a distinction between morality and moralism, noting two forms of the latter: the resort to moral slogans and stereotypes instead of going into the complicated content of moral choice, and the assumption that all problems will yield to moral suasion if only it is pushed with sufficient intensity. Moralism is the stuff of self-righteousness, inspiring propaganda against adversaries and dividing the world into "righteous" and "unrighteous" nations.

The problem with moralistic or religious crusading, according to Bennett, is that it may "make impossible the compromises and accommodations without which nations cannot live together on this planet...

Moralistic foreign policies usually produce devils on the other side, and it is hard to negotiate with devils, though without negotiations there may not be a future for them or for us." In turn, he adds, revulsion against such moralism may lead many critics to avoid all talk about morality in relation to foreign policy.[17]

Frederick Nolde, the first director of CCIA, enumerated the following "dangers of morality":

- The assumption that solutions of international problems can be found solely in moral principles. In most instances effective solutions call for technical and political arrangements for which moral principles primarily provide direction and motivation.
- Ivory tower indulgence. There is need to submit to the discipline of the achievable, always seeking the level of attainability.
- Recourse to morality as a cloak to defend selfish interests. There is need for objectivity in identifying pertinent moral principles and for objectivity in appraising action in the light of them.
- Oversimplification or falsification by classifying actions as right and wrong.
- Concentration solely on the moral substance of a position.[18]

Although the very survival of humanity may be at stake in international relations, this is "an area of most acute difficulty for Christian ethics or for any humane or universal ethics", according to Bennett and Seifert.[19] But if Christian faith and ethics do not produce policy directives for international affairs, they do offer "ultimate perspectives, broad criteria, motives, inspirations, sensitivities, warnings, moral limits", Bennett says.[20]

A Christian perspective

Bennett suggests five elements to "this distinctively Christian perspective".

First, all nations live under the providence, judgement and love of God, "who wills the welfare of each nation as part of the world that he loves, who transcends all nations in such a way that he keeps all their ideals and achievements and ideologies under judgement".[21]

The second element is the commandment of love, which is in fact more than a commandment, because it stems from the demonstration of God's love for all humanity, of which our love at its best is a reflection. The Christian citizen lives under the command of God in Christ to seek the welfare of all neighbours, near and far. Christian love in the hearts of citizens can be translated into the terms of such generally recognized values as justice and order and peace and freedom.

Rather than announcing clear-cut moral laws whose application can be specified in advance, we might speak here of "moral pressures" that remain in force in all situations. Bennett adds, "Let the church in its teaching and liturgy be a source of perpetual reminders of all that is involved in Christian faith and ethics."[22]

The third element is Christian teaching about human nature. The positive side of this is the teaching that human beings are created in the image of God and that this image is renewed in the redemptive work of God through Christ. This, says Bennett, is the Christian basis for both hope and openness to the humanity of people on all sides of any conflict. But there is also another aspect to Christian teaching about human nature: the understanding of human finiteness and sin, "beginning with ourselves".[23]

In the fourth place, says Bennett, the grace of God seeks out the sinner and forgives those who turn to God in faith. This is an essential element of Christian political realism:

> It has enabled Christians to face with full honesty the realities with which they had to live. It has enabled them to live without escape, without self-deception and without despair... There are compromises, those that are inherent in the situation because one value must be sacrificed in part to another and those that stem primarily from our own moral failure. The gospel as understood by Christian realism makes it possible to choose when all possible choices stab the conscience.[24]

The final element which Bennett identifies is the church as an international reality. This is very important for Christians as they face the issue of their country's foreign policy. Being a member of a community whose origins and traditions and authorities are independent of any nation makes a difference in how a Christian relates to his or her own nation, the more so because this Christian community is represented in almost all nations, among people whose experience of life is markedly different from one's own.[25]

Here the words of Jesus about loving one's enemies come out in full force. At first they may strike us as an obligation to be accepted in spite of the facts. Their meaning assumes greater significance, however, when we recognize that the people who may happen to be called enemies are made in God's image and are one with us.

The story is told that when US President Woodrow Wilson visited the Army War College in 1915, he was shocked to find plans being studied there for wars against other countries. While this account (which seems to be a somewhat distorted version of a real episode) is often cited as an example of Wilson's naïveté, it is suggestive of a sensitivity to the phenomenon of "enemy images".

Nations may feel threats from other nations because of differences in philosophy, religion, ethnicity, ideology, competing ambitions, territorial claims or spheres of influence. Inevitably, each will present the other side as the enemy from whom the threat is imminent and permanent.

Nations thus foster enemy images in the name of security. Defense preparedness and defense policy are often directed against a perceived enemy. Enemy images are built on threats, perceptions of threat and the assumption that these are permanent, so that nothing can be done except to build and maintain countervailing if not overwhelming military force.

The ecumenical fellowship has a special responsibility in promoting relationships across "enemy lines" and destroying enemy images, for churches have more possibilities than many other bodies to cultivate such relationships.

An international ethos

The conviction of the significance of the relation between ethics and international affairs and of the valuable contribution churches have to make in this area led the ecumenical movement, as a fellowship of churches from all continents, to recognize from the beginning an international order based on an international ethos as a primary concern.

"To promote friendship between nations" was one of the purposes listed in the official letter of invitation to the Life and Work conference in Stockholm in 1925. Enmity among nations was recognized as a challenge to church unity, and the conference message declared that "the world is too strong for a divided church". Less than 25 years later, the theme of the WCC's first assembly reflected the critical international situation of the time: "Man's Disorder and God's Design".

Introducing the preparatory volume prepared for the first assembly's section on international affairs, CCIA chairman Kenneth Grubb remarked that "the Disorder of Man is to most men nowhere more painfully apparent than in international relations. The Design of God for the Nation is difficult to perceive".[26] While the WCC had no blueprint to offer for the proper functioning of the contemporary world of nations, there was a broad consensus on the desired direction of relations between peoples. It called for a recognition of the sovereignty of God in the ordering of international life by the acceptance of international law administered by supra-national institutions.

As Paul Bock, a scholar of ecumenical social thought, has observed:

> It was apparent that if the church was to perform a prophetic function in the modern world, that is, if it was to serve as a conscience of nations, classes or races — rather than to be an uncritical supporter of any — it would need to have a more universal as well as a more historical perspective. Christians of one nation, in considering a problem, would need to learn how Christians in other nations see it. There are both theological and practical considerations that lead to an ecumenical ethic. Theologically, the Christian faith affirms that the church is one, that it is responding to a God who loves the world and that its members are to be one in manifesting God's love. Practically, it is evident that the world has become one and that the problems of one part directly affect other parts.[27]

It was widely recognized that the church must engage in as rigorous and scientific an analysis as possible of the historical, economic, social and political conditions by which it is surrounded, so that these data could be compared with the biblical record and the signs of renewal attesting to the actual presence of the kingdom it is proclaiming could be recognized. Bieler speaks of "the double aspect of the church's political function, requiring a double method of analysis to formulate its ethics...: scrutinizing the signs of the times and interpreting them in the light of the gospel".[28]

To provide a vision of society that could give some concrete guidance to Christians in the political and social realm has always been an ecumenical concern. The 1937 Life and Work conference in Oxford, in its report on "The Universal Church and the World of Nations", pointed out that development of international law is essential for an international order and argued that "the international church could form the common ethos on which a workable system of international law could be built":

> All law... must be based on a common ethos — that is, a common foundation of moral convictions. To the creation of such a common foundation in moral conviction the church as a supra-national society with a profound sense of the historical realities, and of the worth of human personality, has a great contribution to make.[29]

Reaffirming this judgement, the report of Section IV of the Amsterdam assembly urged support for immediate practical steps on behalf of mutual understanding and goodwill, respect for international law and the development of institutions to deal with questions of international concern on a universal basis.

This concern for international law and its enforcement is linked with an emphasis on the moral foundations which must undergird the rule of law. The theological ground for this concern was stated well by the same report:

> Our Lord Jesus Christ taught that God, the Father of all, is sovereign. We affirm therefore that no state may claim absolute sovereignty, or make laws without regard to the commandments of God and the welfare of mankind. It must accept its responsibility under the governance of God, and its subordination to law within the society of nations. The churches have an important part in laying that common foundation of moral conviction without which any system of law will break down.[30]

The Evanston assembly in 1954 recognized that underlying the more obvious barriers to a genuine world community is the lack of a common foundation of moral principles:

> At the root of the most stubborn conflicts is the failure of governments and peoples to treasure any common set of guiding principles. Attempted settlements involving differing ideologies are essentially unstable and tend to produce new frictions, not only because of political differences but also because of underlying differences as to moral values.[31]

The world of nations desperately needs an international ethos, Evanston said. Providing the necessary sound framework for the development of international law and institutions requires not only attempts to find wider areas of common moral understanding but also efforts to bring the guiding principles of international life into greater harmony with God's will. The assembly advanced two considerations about essential principles:

1. All power carries responsibility, and all nations are trustees of power, which should be used for the common good.
2. All nations are subject to moral law and should strive to abide by the accepted principles of international law, to develop this law and enforce it through common action.[32]

The WCC's New Delhi assembly (1961) again referred to the need for an international ethic and felt that a more profound study of the nature and content of the moral foundations of international law and order would help nations of different traditions to understand and accept their common allegiance to basic ethical conceptions. This call for an international ethic was repeated at the fourth assembly in Uppsala (1968).

A 1981 consultation on political ethics, held as a follow-up of the WCC study on Just, Participatory and Sustainable Society, summarized the challenges well:

> An ecumenical political ethic has to come to terms with the task of discerning the signs of the times, i.e., interpreting the significance of the political events at all levels from a Christian perspective as these affect Christians and churches in their different situations. The ecumenical Christian community responds to the political situation with a special sensitivity to the suffering of people everywhere. In practice, however, Christians respond in different and sometimes extraordinary ways to political events, reflecting different contexts, experiences, interests, fears and hopes. The ecumenical movement has contributed to a sharpening of critical awareness of world political issues among the churches and has drawn them into the difficult task of discerning the signs of the times through mutual exposure and accountability. This is an essential element in any effort in outlining an ecumenical political ethic.[33]

What competence does a body like the World Council of Churches have for translating ethical concerns about international affairs into recommendations on policy and action? To this question we shall turn in the next chapter.

NOTES

[1] Harry D. Davis & Robert C. Good, eds, *Reinhold Niebuhr on Politics*, New York, Scribners, 1960, p.321.
[2] Paul Ramsey, *Who Speaks for the Church?*, Nashville, Abingdon, 1967, p.148.
[3] Stanley Hoffman, *Duties Beyond Borders*, Syracuse, NY, Syracuse University Press, 1981, p.10.
[4] *Ibid.*, p.14.
[5] *Ibid.*, p.18.
[6] *Ibid.*, p.20.
[7] *Ibid.*, p.21.
[8] Max Weber, *Politics as a Vocation*, Philadelphia, Fortress, 1965, p.46.
[9] John C. Bennett & Harvey Seifert, *US Foreign Policy and Christian Ethics*, Philadelphia, Westminster, 1977, p.68.
[10] Weber, *Essays in Sociology*, New York, Oxford University Press, 1958, p.126.
[11] John Habgood, *Church and Nation in a Secular Age*, London, Darton, Longman and Todd, 1983, p.166.
[12] Hoffman, *op. cit.*, p.28.
[13] *Ibid.*, p.32.
[14] *Ibid.*, p.33.
[15] Bennett and Seifert, *op. cit.*, p.29.
[16] *Ibid.*

[17] Bennett, *Foreign Policy in Christian Perspective*, New York, Scribners, 1966, p.18.
[18] O. Frederick Nolde, *The Churches and the Nations*, Philadelphia, Fortress, p.62.
[19] Bennett and Seifert, *op. cit.*, p.15.
[20] Bennett, *Foreign Policy in Christian Perspective*, p.36.
[21] *Ibid.*, p.37.
[22] *Ibid.*, p.39.
[23] *Ibid.*, p.41.
[24] *Ibid.*, p.45.
[25] *Ibid.*, p.47.
[26] *The Church and the International Disorder*, London, SCM Press, 1948, p.13.
[27] Paul Bock, *In Search of a Responsible Society*, Philadelphia, Westminster, 1974, p.20.
[28] André Bieler, *The Politics of Hope*, Grand Rapids, Eerdmans, 1974, p.121.
[29] *The Churches Survey Their Task*, London, Allen and Unwin, 1938, p.173-74.
[30] *The Church and the International Disorder*, p.224.
[31] *The Evanston Report*, New York, Harper, 1955, p.141.
[32] *Ibid.*, p.142.
[33] Koson Srisang, ed., *Perspectives on Political Ethics*, Geneva, WCC, 1983, p.18.

4

Resources and Competence

Amidst the complexity, unpredictability and ambiguity of international affairs, what resources are available to a body like the World Council of Churches for acting in this realm on the basis of its ethical concerns? Certainly, as the 1966 Geneva conference on Church and Society pointed out, there is no set of universally valid rules or easy-to-apply abstract principles. However,

> Holy Scripture, Christian history, contemporary Christian experience and the insights of the social sciences and other secular disciplines do inform the situation, and in their light the Christian is called to be obedient to his understanding of God's will in his particular situation...
>
> The discernment by Christians of what is just and unjust, human and inhuman in the complexities of political and economic change is a discipline exercised in continual dialogue with biblical resources, the mind of the church through history and today, and the best insights of social scientific analysis.[1]

So WCC statements and actions ought to reflect the teachings of the Bible, ecumenical social thought and the best available political analysis. To say this, as M.M. Thomas has pointed out, is not to consider "the complexities of political and economic change" as a new revelation, but to see them "as the continuing work of the living Jesus Christ to awaken man to his true humanity, promised in Christ, and needing the discipline of the gospel for its fulfilment".[2]

John C. Bennett observes that much of what is most relevant to the discussion of contemporary political problems in the history of Christian thought

> is more fundamental and broader than Christian political theory. It deals with God's purpose for our life, with the nature of man and society, with the political symptoms of sin, with the direct and indirect political effects of the

> redemption mediated to us by Christ, with the essential nature of the church and its role in society.[3]

Theological entry points

Warning against the temptation to build Christian political thought on a single doctrinal emphasis, J. Philip Wogaman has identified several significant "theological entry points" to an understanding of politics.

The first is the sovereignty of God. Our ultimate allegiance is to God, and whenever human authority is in clear conflict with divine authority, it is the latter that is sovereign. "In saying that they must obey God rather than human authority (in Acts 5:29) Peter and the other apostles spoke for all Christians everywhere on this matter of ultimate loyalty."[4]

But how are we to know the will of the sovereign God? Wogaman notes that "what appears to some to be a conflict between God and human authority may appear to others as an instance of human authority implementing the will of God". This leads to the second entry point: the transcendence of God. The sovereign God is beyond full human comprehension. This is not to say that one can know nothing about the divine will:

> It would be meaningless to speak of the will of God if there were no basis whatsoever for asserting that any course of action reflects that will; but the transcendence of God injects an element of principled humility into the question.[5]

Human finitude is the third theme suggested by Wogaman. While not denying the enormous capacity and impressive achievements of human beings, one must recognize also that there are things which human beings cannot comprehend. This "reinforces the point that we cannot so easily identify the judgement of any human being or group of people with the will of God".[6]

A fourth entry point — the covenant — is a concept which is at the heart of both the Hebrew and the Christian understanding of God. Expressed in the great moments of Israel's history — the exodus, the giving of the law at Sinai, the entry into the promised land — the covenant reinforces the sovereignty of God and creates the community. And in Jesus Christ we see the depth of God's covenantal love revealed and understand the covenant to be universal.

The political consequence of this inclusive universal community is that "no people can be understood as total aliens, not even clear political adversaries. All political divisions based upon city, nation or empire are relativized by the covenantal notion when it is applied in this universal sense."[7]

Fifth, the theology of the cross. Wogaman says the cross portrays human sin and divine love in the most vivid possible contrast. Translated into relevant political terms, the theology of the cross can point to the contrast between the altogether positive, self-sacrificial expression of love on the cross and the negative uses of violence and coercion in "power politics". In a profound sense, the cross challenges every designation of people as the enemies of God.

Related to the doctrine of the cross is a sixth theme — justification and grace — which focusses on God's love as a free unmerited gift. This has political relevance whenever the question is raised of who deserves a given political benefit. "The concept of grace is a kind of leveller," Wogaman says. "We are all, ultimately, dependent upon God's free gift of love, unmerited, undeserved" — though he concedes that it is difficult to translate this into the details of policy.[8]

Seventh, the doctrine of creation. The belief that the natural universe and its inhabitants were created by God has a number of political consequences. Some of these have long been prominent in discussions of war and peace and economic and political oppression. But the new consciousness of the integrity of creation also has important political implications.

Eighth, original sin. There are three general views of the political consequences of sin. One, associated with Thomas Hobbes, sees human nature as profoundly sinful, leading to the selfish and "immoral" use of power by the government. Another, held by Leo Tolstoy and others, emphasizes human nature as benevolent, leading to peace in society and minimum power of government. But if we take a third view, like Reinhold Niebuhr, and consider all people as sinners while still recognizing the possibilities of goodness in human nature, our view of politics will be a more nuanced one, and "we can seek to develop a political society that protects all against the sinful tendencies of each, while also providing institutional support for the more creative, positive, community-building possibilities to assert themselves".[9]

David Jenkins warns that the doctrine of sin can function as a justification for inaction or indifference:

> To use the perspective on human affairs which is symbolized by the doctrine of Original Sin as an excuse for writing off all human attempts to better one's earthly and social predicament or to reduce all political efforts to the same level of indifferent values is to trivialize the doctrine to the level of a pessimistic slogan which is alarmingly available for that type of conservatism or reaction which interprets realism as licensing acquiescence in the injustices

and distortions of any particular status quo on the grounds that sin is inevitable and ubiquitous.[10]

Ecclesiology and liberation are two other theological themes which have important consequences for politics.

The institution of the church has its own structure and government, which means that issues related to power, responsibility and accountability arise in it. Unhappily, it often seems that instead of providing models and ethical criteria for politics and government, the church takes into its own life the worst of secular practice of power.

A powerful theme is added to the Christian understanding of politics by liberation theologians. The key metaphor they use is the story of the exodus, by which God acted directly to set the Hebrew slaves free from their bondage in Egypt and make them into a nation. This theme of liberation runs centrally through the Old and New Testaments. For the liberation theologians, the exodus is not a separate "religious" event, but points to the deepest meaning of the whole biblical narrative. In this event the dislocation introduced by sin is resolved, and injustice, oppression and liberation are determined. In the New Testament, Wogaman says, "the work of Christ forms part of this movement and brings it to complete fulfilment. The work of Christ therefore brings a liberation that fulfils in an unexpected way the promises of the prophets and creates a new chosen people which this time includes all humanity."[11]

Gustavo Gutiérrez voices the belief of most of the liberation theologians in asserting that the exodus experience is a paradigm of the situation humanity faces today. For people who are in bondage today (economic, social, sexist) can also count on God as the fundamental source of their liberation.

With all these themes and "entry points", it is important to see Christian doctrines as defining initial presumptions and informing and illuminating the details in the political realm, rather than taking them as prescriptive. This is particularly true for those who would maintain that for Christians an important point of entry to politics is Jesus himself, which does not mean seeing Jesus himself as an immediately political figure.

In the words of Ronald Preston, "Jesus' kingdom ethic is continually raising an eschatological question mark against provisional human achievements but without devaluing them".[12] The gospels do not present Christ as a political activist, but as one who calls people to a discipleship that may turn out to be political.

Two kinds of differences may arise in the application of Christian doctrines in the political realm. On the one hand are honest differences in defining initial presumptions even when using the same theological entry points; on the other are differences emerging in a particular situation when different theological entry points give differing, even contradictory signals. Recognizing these difficulties is important in the ecumenical community, especially since differences among churches on politics may also result from diverse confessional approaches to the issue of relations between church and state.

Ecumenical social thought

A second important resource for the involvement of churches in international affairs is the legacy of ecumenical social thought. We have referred in earlier chapters to some aspects of ecumenical thought relating to ethics and international affairs. Here we shall look at the evolution of ecumenical social thought as an important resource for both discernment and the formulation of criteria for actions.

From early times international ecumenical bodies have made pronouncements on social and political issues and described concepts of justice, peace and the like. Such descriptions have often been presented or perceived as visions of society, criteria for society or blueprints for an ideal society. Sometimes in a more limited way they have been presented as a framework or point of coordination for ecumenical programmes. In general, these descriptions have reflected particular stages of evolution of ecumenical social thought.

The evolution of social thought is closely related to the various stages in the ecumenical movement and to changing historical circumstances. One of the formative impulses for the ecumenical movement was an emerging awareness that it is the common task of the churches to contribute to the solution of the problems of modern society; and since its establishment in 1948 the WCC has been a source of inspiration for its member churches towards a greater awareness of this social and political responsibility in the world.

The Life and Work conference in 1925 in Stockholm became the starting point for a new tradition of ecumenical social thought which would develop in the course of the following decades. Here was a convergence of Christian movements in several countries devoted to social justice and world peace.

The message of the conference begins with a call to repentance and an invitation to the churches to dedicate themselves anew under the cross of Jesus Christ to the task of witnessing to the power of his gospel in all realms of life — industry, society, politics and international relations.

The Stockholm message makes it clear that Christian action in and for the world is an integral part of the church's witness to the gospel of Jesus Christ. Paul Bock suggests that "this first phase of the search for an ecumenical social ethic might be called an international social gospel phase. The search at this time was under strong Anglo-Saxon influence and was based on a liberal theology."[13]

The next stage is associated with Life and Work's 1937 Oxford conference on "Church, State and Community", a landmark in ecumenical social thought. The conference met at a bleak period in international life — a time of disillusionment caused by global economic depression, large-scale unemployment, the impotence of the League of Nations and the alarming rise of Nazism, fascism and totalitarian communism.

Preparations for the conference focussed on the relationship of the church to the world. The Oxford report stressed a Christian view of justice derived from the love commandment. In Bock's words:

> It took a realistic view of man and his sinfulness and did not anticipate a utopian society but rather one in which power had to be used to assure justice. The kingdom of God was not viewed as a realizable goal in society but as a concept of the perfect rule of God which draws men forward but which also judges all men's achievements.[14]

As Konrad Raiser points out:

> Central to the thinking at Oxford was a new Christian understanding of the state and the responsible use of power. Oxford arrived at a sober and balanced view of the state as an historical reality serving the common good but, because of the increasing concentration of power and its monopoly of the means of coercion, potentially becoming the instrument of evil.[15]

Since God was seen as the source of justice, the state was considered not the ultimate source of law but its guarantor, not the lord but the servant of justice.

An important contribution of Oxford was the development of guidelines for evaluating a particular social order. These came to be known as "middle axioms". We will consider these in some detail in Chapter 7.

In terms of social thought Oxford prepared the ground for the founding assembly of the WCC in Amsterdam, which took place in the early stages of the cold war. Manifesting the desire to transcend the growing East-West conflict, the organizers of the assembly invited a church leader from the West (John Foster Dulles) and another from the East (Josef Hromádka) to address its section on the church and the international order.

In its report "The Church and the Disorder of Society" Amsterdam offered a description of a responsible society. This concept, which was further clarified at the Evanston assembly in 1954, was extremely useful, especially in the context of the ideological conflict. It not only offered a basis for political ethics but evoked the possibility of new and creative solutions. Amsterdam recognized, as had the Oxford conference in 1937, that there is no Christian social order and that no social order should be identified with the kingdom of God. The concept of a responsible society served as "a criterion by which we judge all existing social orders and at the same time a standard to guide us in the specific choices we have to make", as a later assembly stated. Amsterdam developed a definition of it which sought to balance freedom, order and justice.

> A responsible society is one where freedom is the freedom of men who acknowledge responsibility to justice and public order and where those who hold political authority or economic power are responsible for its exercise to God and the people whose welfare is affected by it.[16]

While the report presented the responsible society as a criterion, it also argued that this must be embodied in political institutions and specified the functions and characteristics of these. The assembly itself referred to the responsible society as a goal for which all the churches in all lands should work.

But the world was moving fast. Ecumenical social thought began in a Western milieu, and both Stockholm and Oxford were basically Western conferences. As the experiences of churches in newly developing countries came to be reflected more and more in ecumenical circles, the concept of responsible society came under challenge. In the 1960s, especially in the context of the WCC studies on "Areas of Rapid Social Change", such challenges came mainly from Asia and Latin America, calling into question the theological, economic and political assumptions underlying the concept of the responsible society. Whereas Western churches still placed great confidence in the traditional global structures for political and economic relations, these new voices criticized the inherent biases of these institutions and the imposition on the rest of the world of an "international law" developed by the Western powers.

The 1966 Geneva conference on Church and Society became the forum in which this challenge was aired. Considerable differences of opinion were evident in its discussion of the "technical and social revolutions of our time". For the first time there was a fundamental critique of the "theology of the responsible society" and an affirmation that development presupposes a radical change of national and international political systems. According to the Geneva report, Christians are called "to speak a radical 'No' — and to act accordingly — to structures of power which perpetuate and strengthen the status quo at the cost of justice to those who are its victims".[17] The idea of a responsible society had to be expanded to include concerns for necessary revolutionary change, rapid social change, the struggle against racism and the legitimacy of certain forms of nationalism.

Representatives of developing countries pointed to the inherent conflict between the social and technological revolutions: without a social revolution, they said, the technological revolution would simply make the rich nations rich faster and widen the gap between the rich and the poor countries.

Raiser views the Geneva conference as both conclusion and new departure and has examined both the continuity and discontinuity with earlier phases of ecumenical social thought.[18]

Most of the themes continue with new dimensions, but the changes are significant. In terms of methodology, Raiser points to the shift "from study to action, translating the consolidated consensus into specific initiatives for change". Especially in the areas of racism and human rights, action-oriented programmes and "action-reflection" processes were prominent in the WCC after the Uppsala assembly in 1968.

Geneva also marked a change in emphasis from a universal approach focussing on structures to a more contextual approach that stressed people and their participation in ongoing struggles. Furthermore, Raiser points to a change in relation to

> the three central elements embraced by the concept of the responsible society: freedom, justice and order. While in the earlier phases the primary emphasis was placed on the concerns for freedom and order, the central notion since the Uppsala assembly has become justice in its economic, social and progressively also its political dimensions; and the concern for freedom is now being expressed in terms of "human dignity".

The WCC's fifth assembly (Nairobi 1975) gave ecumenical social thought a new vision and a new expression: the "just, participatory and sustainable society" (JPSS).

The JPSS study, launched soon after Nairobi, pursued several important areas of enquiry, which offer guidelines for the churches' political engagement:

- interpretation of the world political situation, discerning the signs of the times and the understanding of the biblical tradition in the context of the cultural and religious heritage;
- reaffirmation of the centrality of justice, deepening its explication, and further study of the question of sustainability in relation to the struggle for peace;
- deepening of the analysis and interpretation of power and justice in relation to the various understandings and practices of democracy, with particular emphasis on the concepts of equality and participation;
- Christian responsibility and ecumenical solidarity in facing the structures of political power.

In its report to the WCC central committee in 1979, an advisory committee appointed to oversee the JPSS study said:

> Christians believe that the whole world is God's creation, continuously being renewed by the power of redemption and living under the promise of God's kingdom, the reign of peace and justice. Christians believe that all human beings are part of a dynamic pointing towards the messianic kingdom... They live under a special call to obedience, to engage with other people in a search for the common aim: justice on earth, manifested in peaceful community of all humankind in which every human being finds true fulfilment of life.[19]

In 1981, a WCC consultation in Cyprus on political ethics, a follow-up to the JPSS study, suggested some ethical guidelines for political action by the churches:

- readiness to assist and support victims of political decisions and intervene with government authorities on their behalf;
- going beyond assistance to victims of systematic human rights violations and addressing the root causes and structural origins of these violations;
- bearing witness, "under all circumstances and whatever the given relationship to the political status may be", to the truth, beginning with the transformation of their own life and structures;
- respect for the integrity and dignity of politics.[20]

Further evolution of ecumenical social thought is evident in the statements and reports of the WCC's sixth assembly (Vancouver 1983). In what appeared to be a new historical context, with an unprecedented upsurge in the arms race and heightened international tension, the statements from Vancouver went beyond earlier ones on similar topics and assumed certain new features.

Many of the significant new impulses coming out of Vancouver are summed up in its call to the churches to engage in a "conciliar process of mutual commitment to justice, peace and the integrity of creation" (JPIC). Despite certain confusions and setbacks along the way, the JPIC process stimulated renewed ecumenical involvement in many areas over the succeeding years. A world convocation on JPIC in Seoul in 1990 provided a point of concentration for this process, whose continuing ecumenical significance has been reaffirmed on several occasions by WCC governing bodies.

What was new at Vancouver?

1. What was affirmed about justice, peace and the integrity of creation is more than that they are inter-related. Justice, peace and the integrity of creation form one whole. They are inseparable and indivisible. Earlier WCC statements had affirmed the inter-relationship of justice and peace. But only at Vancouver was the connection of justice and peace made a matter of clear conviction and inescapable fact.

2. It follows that it is one struggle in which we are engaged — for justice, peace and the integrity of creation — although the contexts and thus the emphases may differ. Tensions may even appear in the respective claims of justice, peace and the integrity of creation.

3. The new concept of the "integrity of creation" goes far beyond the earlier concept of sustainability, taking into account the relationship between peace and ecology and emphasizing the threat to the very creation. Above all, it points to an understanding of the wholeness of created life in the world as it is in the plan of God.

4. The assembly's affirmations on nuclear weapons and deterrence, weapons of mass destruction and apartheid were made in almost non-negotiable terms. Beyond being social and political issues, these were dealt with as matters of faith.

5. It follows that the churches' primary approach to these issues is not in terms of programmes or even actions of solidarity. Witness to peace and justice is part of the confession of faith.

6. Linked to this "ecclesiological" dimension is the demand for new forms of unity — in the recognition that at certain points of the struggle the very being (and not only the action) of the church is at stake. That means that the church in faithfulness to the gospel is compelled to render its witness, suffering with the people, irrespective of political effectiveness.

7. The new framework brings to the fore the idea that justice, peace and the integrity of creation are notions intimately linked to the biblical

idea of covenant: for example, justice is behaviour and action that is faithful to the community of covenant; integrity of creation is the state of creation as a subject in its own right within God's covenant.[21]

Analyzing politics

Politics and its consequences are unavoidable facts of human existence; and anyone concerned about choices in politics has to do at least some political analysis. Usually, this analysis is not systematic; it may not even be conscious. In order to clarify how a body like the WCC moves from underlying assumptions drawn from the Bible and from ecumenical social thought to statements, recommendations and actions on political issues, it will be helpful to look more closely at the process of political analysis.

For example, consider a news report that the United Nations has decided to intervene in Bosnia. One may ask at least four questions: What is the situation in Bosnia that warrants intervention? Is such intervention good for the people of Bosnia? What does it mean to say that the UN is intervening? What will be the best policy with regard to Bosnia?

These questions reflect four orientations, which we may call, respectively, empirical, normative, semantic and policy orientations. Empirical analysis seeks to provide knowledge of what is, normative analysis knowledge of what ought to be and policy analysis knowledge of how to proceed from the one to the other.[22]

Semantic analysis, which aims at clarification of meaning, is important in political analysis because many of the key concepts have no commonly accepted definitions. Words like democracy, freedom, justice, order, revolution, coercion, power are used in different ways by political practitioners to suit their convenience. Nor do political scientists and political philosophers agree on what they mean.

It is important to recognize that the knowledge sought by each of these is not completely independent of the others, and, more importantly, that political analysis is never value-free. It requires certain assumptions, which are rarely made explicit in the analysis itself. For the WCC, as we have seen, these assumptions come from biblical insights and ecumenical social thought.

From simple matters at the local level to complex issues of international affairs, human beings have to make choices and take decisions. Churches are not exempt from this human reality; and they usually make political decisions even when they do not necessarily take a public position or action.

These decisions are influenced by what one considers to be the alternative courses of action available; what one believes to be the likely consequences of pursuing each of these alternatives; and what value one assigns to the consequences of each alternative. These three appraisals are the most important ones in situations where one has virtual certainty about the consequences of each alternative. But generally, one cannot be certain of all the consequences; and then guesses, hunches or estimates come into play.[23]

Estimates of consequences can vary; and many disagreements about policy can be traced to precisely such differences in projecting consequences. Two people may agree substantially on the alternatives, the "possible" consequences of each and their evaluation of the different sets of consequences, yet disagree on policy because their estimates concerning the likelihood of these consequences differ.

Semantic analysis seems to have gained prominence in recent political evaluation, perhaps because the international situation is in such flux and the meanings of so many terms — for example, sovereignty, legitimacy, human rights, self-determination, minority — are being debated and even changed.

Strongly influenced by the later work of Ludwig Wittgenstein, semantic analysis seeks the meaning of moral terms as they are actually used in ordinary, non-philosophical language. For example, in a famous discussion of justice in Plato's *Republic*, Thrasymachus argues that people seek power "in conscious pursuit of their self-interest", while Socrates counters that they seek it "in order to achieve the collective good".[24] A semantic analysis of this is as follows:

> Though there is a dispute here, it is not between what is and what ought to be, nor between facts and values... One might say that Thrasymachus is talking about the facts of what people consider just, and Socrates about what they ought to consider just in the light of the meaning of "justice". But the meaning of "justice" depends on the facts of its grammar, so this is a dispute about facts, over the implication of two different kinds of facts. It depends on there being an inconsistency in the grammar of "justice" between what people consider just and what the word "justice" means.[25]

Zeal without knowledge?

It is sometimes said that the only certainty about political life is the prevalence of uncertainty. That is why the biblical insights and ecumenical social thought are so important. They illumine and clarify the grounds on which we stand, the principles to which we commit ourselves, the relations among our principles, the nature of the alternatives we confront and finally which alternative is the best and our reason for believing so.

This is highly relevant to the exercise of the quality of discernment. For discernment, Ronald Preston says,

> we need facts. Some of them will come from our own experience and those with whom we chiefly associate, some from the channels of information open to us as citizens, the press, the radio and the television. Some come from experts, but in the end we still have to judge the experts. We cannot do without them but they alone cannot settle issues.[26]

Some have questioned the competence of the WCC to act and speak on international affairs. Does it know enough? This question is not an illegitimate one. For when the Council speaks on international affairs, its competence is not compared with that of individual churches but with that of secular organizations. A degree of specialization and information about fast-moving events are expected. If the WCC is to be taken seriously when it deals with intergovernmental organizations, governments and non-governmental bodies, it must have the requisite degree of knowledge about the issues it addresses.

That this is sometimes the case is evident. During the transition period towards independence for Namibia, WCC international affairs staff held discussions with those responsible for Namibia at United Nations headquarters. The UN officials mentioned that the reports from the monitoring teams of the WCC and the Lutheran World Federation were faster and more reliable than those coming through UN channels. During meetings of the UN Commission on Human Rights, diplomats often turned to WCC representatives for the latest information on South Africa. When there was discussion in the UN on New Caledonia, many delegates relied on a publication and reports by the Commission of the Churches on International Affairs. The information and analysis were so influential that *Le Monde* reported — mistakenly — that the WCC had two full-time staff working on this issue (there were in fact no special staff working on New Caledonia).

Cases in which the WCC has information to act with special competence are usually those — and there are many — in which the churches are deeply involved. In such situations the WCC tends to speak more often and is listened to more carefully. Other examples which might be cited have related to situations of human rights in Korea, the Philippines and El Salvador, the Armenian genocide, the consequences of nuclear tests in the Marshall Islands and Korean reunification. WCC reports and publications on all these issues were recognized as valuable pieces of information by intergovernmental and non-governmental organizations.

Although the churches are the WCC's special source of information, it gathers data from all available channels. A good deal of information comes from human rights organizations — some church-related, others not; some national, others international. Delegations and teams sent by the WCC to areas of crisis receive and collect valuable data. All this supplements reports received through the print media, radio and television, a careful monitoring of which gives a wealth of information, though sometimes it may be incomplete, inaccurate or slanted.

Preston offers some useful reminders about facts:

> Facts are necessary. But it is more complicated than that. For facts are seen in a context of significance. "Bare" facts by themselves do not help. The selection of what among them are worth attending to and the weightage given to them are determined by our value judgements. These value judgements come from our overall understanding of human life, that is to say our philosophy or our religion. So the Christian will find his faith illuminating the facts, as well as forming his character and inspiring his vision in his task of discernment.[27]

Another pertinent observation on facts comes from Robert McAfee Brown: "Don't wait until all the facts are in before you act. The facts are never all in."[28]

Two other difficulties should be noted here. One is that the relative importance of events is not always reflected in the attention they are given by the media. A good deal of information is often available for events which are reported in headlines — what broadcasters call the "main points of the news". Facts on equally or more important events which are no longer in the headlines are much more difficult to gather.

A more serious problem is posed by disinformation: the deliberate propagation or leaking of misleading information. In times of crisis and on critical issues many governments indulge in this. For example, it is now known that support for the US Strategic Defense Initiative ("Star Wars") in the 1980s was based on fabricated data and manipulation of research. When war breaks out, sophisticated propaganda operations go into effect, so that, in the familiar phrase, truth is often "the first casualty".

Hand in glove with disinformation are government claims that it alone is in possession of certain information, which it cannot reveal since this would not be in the public interest. Only years later, if ever, is such information available to the public. This makes evaluation and judgement of government policies on foreign affairs very difficult for the public. In foreign affairs, especially on defense-related matters, governments often use a language of secrecy and threat. In fact information is often "classified" by governments largely to avoid transparency, public accountability and embarrassment.

All governments have intelligence agencies which gather a great deal of information — some of it through covert operatives and sophisticated technological means — which is not made available to the public. Although the main sources of information for these agencies are in fact open and accessible to everyone, it is in the selection of such information and its analysis to suit certain political purposes that these intelligence agencies flourish.

John Le Carré, well known for his novels about intelligence agents, has made some pertinent comments on how information is gathered by such agencies. One reason that intelligence assessments are so frequently distorted, he says, is that a single source can produce "a whole lot of seemingly separate intelligence documents", through leaks, clandestine contacts and intercepted messages. Thus what is taken as confirmation of intelligence already received may often be different versions of the same original report.

"One of the great intelligence debacles of the cold war was the overestimation of the Soviet Union's capabilities," John Le Carré says.

> I think it was a failure of intelligence and, in a curious way, a failure of common sense. The overkill of coverage was so immense that they literally started counting the cows twice. When you have huge amounts of data coming in, it's very easy to lose count as simply as that. But the failure of common sense is absolutely weird in its stupidity. Any good journalist who had been living in Moscow in the later years of Brezhnev would know that nothing worked any more. The Knight was dying in his armour, and somehow that human perception never made itself felt in intelligence analysis.[29]

Although in principle top-level statesmen have full access to all information available to their governments, in practice they get only a part of it. By the time information reaches them, it has become so condensed and separated from reality that it often leads to complete misinterpretation of the situation. Joseph Frankel points out that the interpretation of information "is not fully rational but is often governed by emotions, by the tendency in people to develop 'blind spots' for what is unpleasant and by wishful thinking". He continues:

> What we find out about our environment is thus so remote from reality that instead of speaking about knowledge we should employ rather the word

> "image". The important feature of an image is its emphasis on the general outline rather than detailed items of information. Once a statesman has formed an image of an issue or of another state, this image acts as an organizing device for further information and as a filter through which this information must pass. Images, not detailed information, govern political behaviour. Voters tend to be swayed by the image of the party rather than by specific electoral issues; statesmen deal with another state on the basis of their image of this state rather than on the merits of the concrete problem on hand. The ingrained respective images of a hostile superpower governed the mutual relations of the Americans and the Russians much more than the details of their actual behaviour. When this behaviour does not correspond with the image, it is simply ignored.[30]

Modern communications technology, particularly television images beamed by satellites around the globe, reduce the capacity of governments to sift information gathered through traditional channels and formulate foreign policy at a leisurely pace. Television pictures of Kurds in northern Iraq after the Gulf War and of factional strife aggravating famine in Somalia played a major role in determining US government policies in these places. This is an important new element with a direct influence on foreign policy decision-making.

One reason international issues may be complex is due to technical elements which require specialized knowledge. It is true that a body like the WCC does not always have such technical knowledge, but once it is acknowledged that such knowledge is not the exclusive monopoly of governments, access to it through experts is possible. Within the WCC constituency there is a great deal of expertise on the different situations and issues it deals with in international affairs.

M.M. Thomas has pointed to the moral significance of technical decisions:

> In the modern world it is impossible to conceive of any particular moral or Christian responsibility in politics, economics or society without involving ourselves in technical problems which are rarely simple and clear. One may go further and say that it is in the technical decisions that one is moral or immoral and Christian or non-Christian. And without an understanding of the technical issues that are involved in the field in which Christians are called to act responsibly, mere goodwill or even piety does not go far.[31]

A caution against simplistic judgements comes from Philip Potter, former general secretary of the WCC:

> Christians and the churches have been enlightened and enriched by researches in the social and economic sciences and in the tough analysis of

> society which have developed in the last hundred years. We are no longer permitted to indulge in simplistic judgements about ourselves and society.[32]

To this should be added John Bennett's salutary qualification about experts:

> Whenever we deal with any kinds of experts in the political or social sciences, it is important to consider not only the contribution of their superior knowledge but also the presuppositions that determine the use of such knowledge. One protection is to be exposed to a variety of experts with different presuppositions.[33]

The assumptions and presuppositions of the experts may of course be influenced by their scientific expertise but cannot be solely attributed to it. Still, these assumptions determine the kinds of policy recommendations the experts make. So, as Preston says, "in the end we will have to judge the experts". Experience, including that of the immediate victims, should qualify expertise. It is the perspective of the people in the struggles for human rights, justice and peace that should decide the policies of the World Council of Churches. The closer to them the Council is, the more competent it will be.

NOTES

[1] *World Conference on Church and Society, Official Report*, Geneva, WCC, 1967, pp.111,201.

[2] M.M. Thomas, *Towards a Theology of Contemporary Ecumenism*, Madras, CLS, and Geneva, WCC, 1978, p.164.

[3] John C. Bennett, *Christians and the State*, New York, Scribners, 1958, pp.xvi-xvii.

[4] J. Philip Wogaman, *Christian Perspectives on Politics,* London, SCM, 1988, p.114.

[5] *Ibid.*, p.115.

[6] *Ibid.*, p.116.

[7] *Ibid.*, pp.117-18.

[8] *Ibid.*, p.119.

[9] *Ibid.*, p.120.

[10] David Jenkins, "Doctrines which Drive One to Politics", in *Christian Faith and Political Hopes*, London, Epworth, 1979, p.149.

[11] Wogaman, *op cit.*, p.54.

[12] Ronald H. Preston, *Christian Ethics and the Political Order*, London, SCM, 1987, p.173.

[13] Paul Bock, *In Search of a Responsible World Society*, Philadelphia, Westminster, 1974, p.35.

[14] *Ibid.*, p.37.

[15] Konrad Raiser, in *Perspectives on Political Ethics*, ed. Koson Srisang, Geneva, WCC, 1983, p.2.

[16] *The First Assembly of the World Council of Churches*, London, SCM, 1949, p.77.

[17] *World Conference on Church and Society, Official Report*, Geneva, WCC, 1967, p.20.

[18] Raiser, *loc. cit.*, pp.4-5.

[19] In *Perspectives on Political Ethics*, p.178.

[20] *Ibid.*, p.28.

[21] Ninan Koshy, "The WCC and Justice, Peace and the Integrity of Creation", JPIC resource materials 1.4.

[22] Robert A. Dahl, *Modern Political Analysis*, Englewood Cliffs, NJ, Prentice-Hall, 1984, p.12-14.

[23] *Ibid.*, p.129.

[24] Quoted by Dahl, *ibid.*, p.112.

[25] Hannah Fenichel Pitken, *Wittgenstein and Justice*, Berkeley, University of California Press, 1972, p.187.

[26] Ronald H. Preston, *Church and Society in the Late Twentieth Century*, London, SCM, 1983, p.105.

[27] *Ibid.*, pp.105-106.

[28] Robert McAfee Brown, "The Experience of the 60s: A Few Lessons", *Christian Century*, 3-10 January 1979, p.7.

[29] Interview in *Time*, 5 July 1993, p.32.

[30] Joseph Frankel, *International Relations*, London, Oxford University Press, 1969, pp.40-41.

[31] M.M. Thomas, *Christian Participation in Nation Building*, Bangalore, CISRS, 1964, p.297.

[32] Quoted by Preston, *op cit.*, p.108.

[33] John C. Bennett & Harvey Seifert, *US Foreign Policy and Christian Ethics*, Philadelphia, Westminster, 1977, p.67.

5

The Church, Nationalism and the International Fellowship

State and nation

When we use the term "international relations" what we are actually talking about is interstate relations. The United Nations is an interstate body or, more precisely, an intergovernmental body. However, the word "state" in English has no commonly used adjective form that conveys the political sense of the term. (There is the word "stately", but matters of state are often not what would be described as "stately".) So we use the more flexible term "national", and speak of "international relations" and "international law" and refer to a state's acquisition of industrial or commercial enterprises as "nationalization".

It is, however, important to bear in mind the distinctions and relations between a state and a nation. Since the French Revolution, nationalism has been the main spiritual and emotional force cementing all the elements of statehood into nation-states, which have become the typical political unit. Wherever the nation-state is a reality, nationalism buttresses and reinforces existing multinational states.

Not every nation has its own state. There may be several nations in one state. A nation may be divided among two or more states. Historically speaking, the close links between state and nation are relatively recent, and they are subject to change with the evolution of states and nations.

The links between states and nations vary greatly in time and place. Sometimes states precede nations as in Western Europe; sometimes nations precede states as in Central and Eastern Europe; sometimes multinational states and nations with large majorities are formed. All these formations develop their own particular characteristics.

Joseph Frankel points out that it is possible to define a nation according to either the objective characteristics shared by its individual members or their subjective sentiments. An objective definition appears in a 1939 report by the Royal Institute of International Affairs, which found the following features in most nations:

- the idea of a common government, either as a past or present reality or as a future aspiration;
- a certain size and closeness of contact between all individual members;
- a more or less defined territory;
- certain characteristics — often language — that distinguish it from other groups;
- certain interests common to all individual members;
- a certain degree of common feeling or will associated with the members' image of the nation.

A subjective definition describes nationalism as a "state of mind". Frankel cites Renan's 1882 description of the nation as a "soul, a spiritual principle", whose existence is a "daily plebiscite".[1]

With the debate about nation-states and nationalism taking on renewed prominence in international affairs, it may be useful to review the biblical insights into nations. A survey of Old Testament passages concerning God and the nations is provided by Lionel Whiston, who summarizes this in four propositions:

1. All nations exist under God's sovereignty and are subject to God's purposes for all humanity. We must therefore give up any provinciality and seek to understand the role of every nation and people upon earth in terms of God's purposes for it.

2. A nation must be a people under God and dwell in the world as a people among peoples. The Old Testament writers use two Hebrew terms for social groupings: *am* to represent the essential kinship of a group, and *goy* to represent the idea of nationhood. A nation comes under divine judgement when the excesses of nationalism lead it to forget its kinship with all other peoples.

3. God is determined that all people and all nations know that God alone is supreme and that God's will shall be done on earth. Tensions and estrangement among nations reveal both national sin and divine judgement.

4. The people of God are to be a witness to the nations. We must think through what this means in our present situation and ask ourselves to what form of suffering we have been called.[2]

A cardinal principle for Christians to remember in dealing with international affairs is that God has no favourite among nations. God's love extends to all people and all nations are judged by God's righteousness. In the words of Bennett and Seifert:

> The love of God for all humanity is an inspiration, a guide and a source of judgement for churches and Christians as they relate themselves to the developments in the international scene and the foreign policies of their nations. Christians' hope for the nations depends upon the belief in the unity of humanity as created in the image of God and as the object of God's redemption in Christ.[3]

The sometimes implicit Old Testament theme of the essential kinship of all humanity under God is made clear and explicit in Paul's words to the Athenians, recorded in Acts 17:26: "From one (blood) he made all nations to inherit the whole earth, and he allotted the times of their existence and the boundaries of the places where they would live."

Church and state

Bearing in mind the distinction between nations and states, let us turn to the different approaches taken by churches in various traditions to states and governments. The report of a 1978 WCC colloquium on church and state outlines five such theological options. Of course, no doctrinal concept of church-state relations develops in a vacuum. It is invariably shaped and applied according to historical and cultural elements.

1. *The transfiguring relationship of church and state* (the Orthodox view). The liturgy is the anticipation of the eschatological kingdom, "a going home" in the midst of a sinful world. It is also the central way in which, through the intervention of the believing community, the whole people or nation is sanctified. This continuous intervention of the faithful and the saints of all ages draws all the people into the redeeming grace of God. The central task to which the church is called can thus be expressed in the term *theosis*, that is, growth into sanctification and deification.

This "transfiguring" view of the relation of church and state enables the Orthodox churches to come to grips with a great variety of states. Basically, wherever the freedom to celebrate the liturgy is granted, the church can and will readily support whatever actions the state undertakes to improve the well-being of its people. If this freedom is denied, the Orthodox church is faced with a situation of persecution.

2. *The collaborative relationship of church and state*. In the Roman Catholic tradition and in some Anglican churches, we encounter a concept of church and state, ideally speaking, as two *societates perfectae*

— the former eternal, the latter temporal. They do not stand in opposition but overlap each other. The state exists to provide an ordering framework for the people under the general guidance of natural law and the God-given power of reason. However, since it is subject to sin, the state is in constant need of enlightenment by faith, which the church, in its worship, teaching and mission, is called to provide. Fundamentally, this enables church and state to collaborate.

3. *The antagonistic relationship of church and state*. This tradition, which originated in the Anabaptist movement during the Reformation period, is of considerable significance today. The relationship of church and state is critical and antagonistic, with little room for tolerance, let alone co-operation. Instead, we find a heavy emphasis on conflict. As a community of messianic protest, the church will find itself in constant danger of persecution.

4. *The complementary relationship of church and state* (the Lutheran view). Historically, the Lutheran tradition has evolved in contrast to both the Catholic model of co-operation and the Anabaptist emphasis on protest, using the model of "two kingdoms" or realms, which distinguishes between the two powers by which God on the one hand conserves the world and on the other evangelizes it by his word of grace. Church and state are thus seen as complementary.

5. *The inspirational and transforming relationship of church and state*. On this view, church and state are corresponding entities, related to each other as two more or less concentric spheres, each subject to the kingship of Christ over all creation. Their offices remain clearly distinct, but the mandate of each in its respective realm is to bear fruit, knowingly and unknowingly. The church has the inspirational and transforming task of reminding the state that it is not autonomous. There is here the constant tension of the eschatological dimension inspiring and penetrating the ordering of human affairs.[4]

This classification is not exhaustive. For example, it does not include the fundamentalist tradition or the tradition of a national church, both of which have significant influence today. Moreover, within many traditions there is an overlapping and mixture of these approaches. Transfiguration and transformation may go together; the distinction between collaboration and complementarity may be narrow; and the protest element may influence all the traditions in times of persecution and suffering.

But the ecumenically significant point which emerges from this is the need to remain aware of differences in approach to church-state issues among the variety of confessions held together in the ecumenical fellowship, for these different approaches lead to differences in how churches perceive situations and what they can do about them. Thus different styles may be required in dealing with political issues in different countries.

In addition to different theological understandings of the church-state relationship, there are also different patterns that exist on a juridical or an ideological basis. A 1986 United Nations study on religious intolerance and discrimination identified eight such patterns, on the basis of information supplied by governments:

(a) state religions
(b) established churches
(c) neutral or secular as regards religion
(d) no official religion
(e) separation of church from state
(f) agreements with the Roman Catholic Church
(g) protection of legally-organized religious groups
(h) millet system.[5]

Useful as it is, this classification too is subject to several qualifications. There may be overlapping between the categories of state religion and established church. Separation of church from state can result in a neutral or secular state. The millet system, at least in the traditional sense, does not exist today.

National interests

It is significant that in all these patterns even those churches which are critical of the domestic policies of their government will often hesitate to criticize its foreign policies. If the church is in a minority situation, it may feel vulnerable to charges of disloyalty if it criticizes foreign policy; if it is in a majority situation, it will often feel obliged to be the defender of national interests. In either case, foreign policy seems to be the area in which patriotism has to be proved.

In his classic study *Moral Man and Immoral Society*, Reinhold Niebuhr observes that the very loyalty and altruism of individual citizens, which give them personal moral satisfaction, tend to support the nation's most characteristic sins, powerful ambitions, greed and will to power. "Patriotism transmutes individual unselfishness into national egoism... Perhaps the most significant moral characteristic of a nation is hypocrisy... and this hypocrisy is the tribute which immorality pays to morality."[6]

Usually this is all in the name of "national interests". When nations act and react in the international realm, it is often in terms of what they call vital interests or national security. In the name of patriotism, citizens are called to defend national interests, and the loyalty of those who raise critical questions is doubted.

Participation in the international ecumenical fellowship obliges the churches to look at national interests in terms of how the pursuit of these will affect the interests of people living in other nations and how efforts for common security can be pursued.

The concept of national interests is an ambiguous one, involving differences in perception as well as gaps between perceptions and realities. Thus its relation to morality is a complicated one, whether we are talking about Christian morality or a more broadly based humanistic morality.

National interests are not to be equated with crude nationalism or a fundamentally selfish outlook on the world. All states have legitimate national interests. In the deepest sense, these are the interests of the people in the nation. This recognizes the reality of the nation as political power centre. Problems arise, however, when national interest is identified with the interests of the ruling elite or when the perceived national interests jeopardize the genuine long-range interests of one's own nation or the interests of other nations. Thus war is often pursued and justified in the name of national interest.

During the cold war the term "vital interests" was often used. These vital interests can apparently be anywhere, without any geographical limits, and are so vague and all-encompassing that virtually any action a nation takes in any part of the world, covert or overt, can be justified in their name.

US President Jimmy Carter warned in his State of the Union Address in 1980 that "an attempt by any outside force to gain control of the Persian Gulf region will be regarded as an assault on the vital interests of the USA. A second assault will be repulsed by any means including military force." The Gulf War in 1991 dramatically demonstrated the belief of the US government that it had vital interests in this region. Its continuing reluctance about military intervention in Bosnia might be seen as implying that it has no "vital interests" there, leading some cynics to suggest that what "vital interests" really means is oil.

Another term frequently heard is "strategic interests", which obviously construes national interest in terms of defense and military matters. But the defense can be of vital interests, which as we have seen can be anywhere.

Niebuhr writes that

> "national interests" accurately describes the dominant motive of autonomous nation-states. But all nations are involved in a web of interests and loyalties. Their problem, therefore, is to choose between their own immediate, perhaps too narrowly conceived, interest and common interests of their alliance, or more ultimately of their civilization, in which of course their "national interest" is also involved.[7]

Precisely because "national interest" is often elevated to the status of a high moral principle, the moral issue here becomes all the more important. The root of the matter, seen theologically, is that our objective should be global interest — even more, that our interest has a cosmic dimension. As Wogaman says, "a moral conception of international politics that does not begin with the centrality and universality of God can hardly claim to be Christian".[8]

National security

Related to national interest — and often more problematic — is the term national security. This again is a legitimate concept. National security identifies the nation as a unit to be preserved or secured. The traditional use of the term equated it with defense. But new connotations, reflecting new doctrines, have drastically changed the meaning of the old term "security"; and it is interesting to note that now there are countries with both a ministry of national security and a ministry of defense, suggesting that the two are not the same. Moreover, for countries which form part of a military alliance, national security expands to include the security of all countries belonging to the alliance. So the term is no longer limited to the classic sense linked to the integrity of national boundaries.

Even in the more restricted sense of the term "national security", one ought to ask what or whom a government is seeking to secure, against what kind of a threat and by what means. It is much more difficult to arrive at a consensus as to what constitutes a legitimate threat.

The term "national security" gained currency near the end of the second world war, when the USA developed a new basic theory to explain its relation to the rest of the world. Walter Lippman's best-seller *US Foreign Policy: Shield of the Republic*, published in 1943, argued that the "ideal of peace" and the "unearned security" of the geographical position of the US had "diverted attention from the idea of national security".[9] In a speech in 1945, a War Department planner listed some basic requirements of national security: a much-expanded intelligence service, "national realism", allowing all-out preparations for war on the basis of "aggressive intent" in another nation, and the ability to mobilize for war speedily. "I only wish that we had more apostles to carry the gospel of national security," a senior military officer is reported to have said in response.[10]

In fact, this "gospel" was accepted enthusiastically by most nations on either side of the East-West divide. It then took a truly "national" turn inward. According to the new doctrine, internal subversion came to be seen as the most important threat to national security. The main front is the internal front; and a latent and permanent war exists between the state and a section of the people identified as the enemy. This has led to militarization in a number of countries, especially in Latin America, Africa and Asia. In some countries national security has become an ideology encompassing all spheres of national activity, which actually militates against true security of the people.

Speaking at the second special session of the UN general assembly devoted to disarmament, former WCC general secretary Philip Potter stated:

> International security is indivisible. There can be no security for any unless there is security for all. Any nation which seeks security by destroying or threatening to destroy another nation or people is deluding itself. The security of powerful nations cannot be achieved by destabilizing the political, economic and social structures of other nations. The cause of security is not maintained by humiliation of nations or brutality to people. Security has to be sought in mutual trust and respect between nations, in enabling people to participate fully in the life of their nations, and across national borders, and in cooperation between nations and peoples for peace with justice for all.[11]

The link between justice and security was underlined by the WCC's Vancouver assembly in 1983:

> The blatant misuse of the concept of national security to justify repression, foreign intervention and spiralling arms budgets is of profound concern. No nation can pretend to be secure so long as others' legitimate rights to sovereignty and security are neglected or denied. Security can therefore be achieved only as a common enterprise of nations but security is also inseparable from justice. A concept of "common security" of nations must be reinforced by a concept of "people's security". True security for the people demands respect for human rights, including the right to self-determination, as well as social and economic justice for all within every nation, and a political framework that would ensure it.[12]

Sovereignty and legitimacy

Two other important issues related to states are receiving renewed attention in recent international discussions: sovereignty and legitimacy.

Sovereignty has been described as the "supreme political characteristic" or "the central legal formula" of international society. Historically, the term was originally attached to the person of the chief of state (the sovereign), for the reigning monarch was seen as the embodiment of the collective will of the whole community. But it was recognized that the emperor's power, absolute as it often was, still existed by the implied consent of the citizenry.

Sovereignty in the international context is usually regarded as having three major components: external independence, internal autonomy and territorial integrity.

In recent years a shift in emphasis has taken place in international law with regard to sovereignty. As Michael Reisman points out:

> International law is still concerned with the protection of sovereignty, but in the modern sense the object of protection is not the power base of the tyrant who rules directly by naked power or through the apparatus of a totalitarian political order, but the continuing capacity of a population freely to express and effect choices about the identities and policies of its governors.
>
> In international law, sovereignty can be violated as effectively and ruthlessly by an indigenous as by an outside force, in much the same way that the wealth of natural resources of a country can be spoliated as thoroughly and effectively by a native as by a foreigner.[13]

The moral issue of the legitimacy of governments has also been prominent in recent international discussions. Traditionally, a government's international legitimacy and its ability to represent a state are based on its effective rule over the population in a territory. But an important exception was made by the international community in the case of South Africa. Here a parallel between domestic and international legitimacy was applied. The morally bankrupt policy of apartheid rendered the government illegitimate. On this interpretation, a government must respect the human rights of its people in order to be considered legitimate.

A WCC consultation on South Africa held in Lusaka, Zambia, in May 1987 argued that "civil authority is instituted of God to do good, and under the biblical imperative all people are obliged to do justice and show special care for the oppressed and the poor. It is this understanding that leaves us with no alternative but to conclude that the South African regime is illegitimate". A civil authority becomes illegitimate at the point at which it becomes tyrannical and fails in the obligations which derive from its institution. Similarly, the *Kairos Document*, published by a group of South African theologians in 1985, said "a tyrannical regime has no 'moral legitimacy'. It may be the *de facto* government and it may even be recognized by other governments and therefore be the *de jure* or legal government. But if it is a tyrannical regime, it is from a moral and theological point of view illegitimate."

There are some indications that the international community is ready to extend to other cases the principle of respect for human rights as necessary for legitimacy. A UN general assembly resolution on 10 October 1991 condemned the illegal replacement of the constitutionally elected president of Haïti Jean-Bertrand Aristide and demanded his immediate reinstatement. Among those voting for this resolution were some delegates representing governments which had themselves come to power by a military overthrow of a constitutionally elected government. Thus the regime in Haïti which replaced Aristide, though it apparently had effective control over the territory, was deemed internationally illegitimate.

Moreover, it appears that in recognizing states and having diplomatic relations, moral legitimacy is increasingly being taken into account.

Nationalism today

A significant and complex new debate on nationalism on the international agenda has followed the break-up of the Soviet Union, Yugoslavia and Ethiopia. A strong resurgence of nationalism seems to threaten multinational states, leading to international conflicts of which the atrocities in Bosnia are only the most regular reminder. If Eritrea is seen as the belated solution to a colonial problem, the national questions of the present day are mainly located in the traditional home of national causes — Europe.

The prominent European historian E.J. Hobsbawm has argued that the new outburst of nationalism in Europe has its historical roots in the early twentieth century and that "the explosive issues of 1988-92 were created in 1918-21". National tensions, he notes, remained under effective control as long as the central party operated. But when the Soviet regime withdrew military support from its satellite regimes, the foundations of the independent communist regimes in Balkan Europe were undermined. "Nationalism was the beneficiary of these developments but not in any serious sense an important factor in bringing them about."[14]

Conflicts created by the aspirations and apprehensions of ethnically based nationalism have become the major source of current international tension. Without going into detail about the various reasons for this upsurge of conflicts, we may note a comment by Myron Weiner which sheds important light on the relation between ethnicity and state:

> In country after country, a single ethnic group has taken control over the state and used its power to exercise control over others. In retrospect there has been far less "nation-building" than many analysts had expected or hoped, for the process of state-building has rendered many ethnic groups devoid of power or influence.[15]

In discussing the state and ethnicity one must take account of how patterns of cultural pluralism in a society influence the composition of the elite, national ideology and the institutional structure of the state, as well as the consequences of the character of the state on the development of ethnic consciousness.

Situations in which ethnicity and religion are coterminous are especially volatile at a time of resurgence of religions. While ethnic conflicts are not religious conflicts, the visible presence of religion makes analysis difficult. When church or confessional affiliation is coterminous with ethnicity, the witness of the church is made especially difficult. Movements for religious nationalism profess to aim at strengthening national identities. In a plural society, the result is invariably disruption and often violent upheaval. In many situations religious nationalism has become a threat to the secular state.

The identification of churches and denominations with ethnic nationalities and the political conflicts which misuse these identities have become new threats to the international fellowship of the churches and a challenge to the ecumenical movement.

Part of the vocation of the ecumenical movement has always been to encourage and enable churches to transcend narrow loyalties to their nation and ethnic group. But at the moment it appears that such loyalties are endangering communities and causing divisions. Reflecting on the first two decades of the WCC, Visser 't Hooft wrote:

> The experience of these years shows how difficult it is for the churches to rise above the necessarily limited viewpoint of their national and social environment, but it has also shown that it is precisely through the ecumenical encounter that the necessary mutual correction can take place so that the churches can arrive at a more objective judgement concerning the road to true peace and justice.[16]

NOTES

[1] Joseph Frankel, *International Relations*, London, Oxford University Press, 1972, pp.13-14.

[2] Lionel A. Whiston, Jr., "God and the Nations: A Study in Old Testament Theology", in *Biblical Realism Confronts the Nation*, ed. Paul Peachey, Scottdale, PA, Fellowship Publications, 1963, pp.63-67.

[3] John C. Bennett & Harvey Seifert, *US Foreign Policy and Christian Ethics*, Philadelphia, Westminster, 1977, p.21.

[4] *Church and State: Opening a New Discussion*, Geneva, WCC, 1978, pp.168-171.

[5] Elizabeth Odio Benito, *Study on the Current Dimensions of the Problems of Intolerance and Discrimination on Grounds of Religion and Belief*, Geneva, UN Commission on Human Rights, 1986, p.19.

[6] Quoted by John C. Bennett, *Foreign Policy in Christian Perspective*, New York, Scribners, 1977, p.13.

[7] Reinhold Niebuhr, *The Structure of Nations and Empires*, New York, Scribners, 1959, p.277.

[8] J. Philip Wogaman, *Christian Perspectives on Politics*, London, SCM, 1988, p.265.

[9] Quoted by Daniel Yergin, *Shattered Peace*, New York, Penguin, 1977, p.194.

[10] *Ibid.*, p.195.

[11] *The Churches in International Affairs: Reports 1979-1982*, Geneva, WCC, 1983, p.49.

[12] David Gill, ed., *Gathered for Life: Official Report, VI Assembly, WCC*, Geneva, WCC, 1983, pp.133-34.

[13] Michael Reisman, "Sovereignty and Human Rights in Contemporary International Law", *American Journal of International Law*, Vol. 84, 1990, p.866.

[14] E.J. Hobsbawm, *Nations and Nationalism since 1780*, Cambridge University Press, 1992, p.167.

[15] Myron Weiner, "Political Change: Asia, Africa and the Middle East", in Weiner and Huntington, eds, *Understanding Political Development*, Boston, Little, Brown, 1987, pp.36-37.

[16] W.A. Visser 't Hooft, "The General Ecumenical Development since 1948", in Harold E. Fey, ed., *A History of the Ecumenical Movement*, Vol. 2, Geneva, WCC, 1983, p.23.

6
Ecumenical Diplomacy

The term "diplomacy" normally refers to behaviour and political strategy with regard to foreign affairs on the part of official government representatives. But one can widen the sense of the term and speak of "non-governmental" or "private" diplomacy as well.

In this chapter we will look at what may be called "ecumenical diplomacy" — the styles, models and methodologies used by the World Council of Churches in international affairs.

Areas of concern

The major areas of concern for the WCC in international affairs may be generally identified as follows:

- *peace and justice*, including disarmament and socio-economic justice; a broader framework for this has come through the programme emphasis on Justice, Peace and the Integrity of Creation;
- *conflict situations*, both international and national (the borderline between the two is thin), as well as dormant conflicts and situations which are likely to lead to conflicts;
- *human rights*, conceptual clarifications, response to particular situations and an emphasis on religious liberty;
- *racism*, where the longtime special emphasis on Southern Africa is giving way to a closer look at manifestations of racism in other situations around the world.[1]

Such a categorization, which in no way exhausts the themes on which the WCC works, will be misleading if one fails to recognize that these issues are all inter-related and intertwined, so that more often than not dealing with one of these issues means touching several of the others as well.

> These concerns expressed in contemporary terms emerge out of the biblical image/vision of shalom. Shalom is a condition of wholeness and harmony, of peace, justice and righteousness, of healing and salvation, of freedom, prosperity and well-being. This concept stands in stark contrast to the many conditions of life in which we find ourselves today and which are the results of injustice, oppression, racism, conflict and war. While there is no biblical blueprint for a foreign or global policy, the vision of shalom is ever placed before us as a challenge and as a possibility, and God continues to stir up people who take fresh initiatives and help create the conditions of peace as envisioned in shalom.[2]

Earlier, we mentioned the different levels or dimensions of the WCC — as a council of churches, a frontier movement and an international organization. This combination of roles affects the style of ecumenical diplomacy, for there is a way of functioning and models of action suitable for each. These models and methods have evolved from the experiences of the WCC as well as of churches engaged in the same issues and non-governmental organizations active within the UN system.

The particular demands made by a specific issue and the possibilities in a given situation determine the appropriate methodology. Here the different patterns of church-state relations play a major role. A church's problems, sensitivities and potential to act will depend largely on its tradition, theological approach and actual relations with the government in power. Crucial factors on the side of the state are its ideological stance, policies on religions, attitude to the churches and international pressure.

A church may not have a tradition of taking a critical public stance. Or it may leave itself vulnerable if it criticizes the state openly. It may have other ways to make representations to the government. A state may dismiss all public opinion outside the country as hostile propaganda.

Approaches to a government can be public or confidential. The former may be a condemnation, a criticism or an appeal; the latter is most likely an appeal. In a conflict situation attempts can be made to start mediation and negotiations. Here, too, a broad range of options is available. The judgement as to the most suitable form of action demands a high degree of sensitivity to the situation of the church and the state and the issues concerned — and in arriving at this judgement mistakes can be made and there will often be honest differences of opinion.

Consulting the churches

In deciding on the form of action with regard to the situation in or related to a country, the WCC consults with its member churches. The document *The Role of the WCC in International Affairs* elaborates on this:

> Consultation is a continuous process within the fellowship. Sometimes discussion on specific developments may not be necessary. In some situations such discussion may not be possible or advisable.
>
> Consultation does not mean that the WCC can and should act only with the concurrence of the official bodies of the church or churches in a national situation. Under certain circumstances the WCC hears conflicting voices coming from the church. The assessment made from a global perspective may differ from a national one. When differences occur, careful prior assessment has to be made about the effect of WCC action. Possible disagreement between a church and other churches or with the international body need not be avoided but must be accepted as a necessary consequence of exercising the obligation of discernment as well as that of mutual challenge for renewal in the spirit of the fellowship. It is recognized that some churches may not consider socio-political engagement as part of their mission and that others are engaged in ways considered to be more relevant to their particular situations.[3]

The continuous process of consultation with churches is undergirded by the WCC's active engagement with them. For example, the Council's long involvement in several Latin American situations, South Africa, the Philippines and Korea means that it can legitimately claim to know the mind of the church, and when information is received about new developments, usually from church sources, it may be possible to decide on an appropriate form of action without further immediate consultations.

In some situations it is not feasible or advisable to consult the church concerned before taking action. Recent advances in communication technology have changed the situation to a certain extent, but do not resolve some basic difficulties. In critical situations, a church may come under very close surveillance by the government, so that it may harm the church's interests if it is known to have suggested a particular course of international action or even advised the WCC about the situation.

Soon after the 1974 military coup in Ethiopia which overthrew Emperor Haile Selassie, sixty former military officials were summarily executed without trial by the new regime. When the news reached the outside world there were many enquiries from churches, governments and others about how the WCC would react. Consulting the churches in Ethiopia was out of the question: already under pressure from the new government, they were in no position to comment on the events or give advice.

In a statement the general secretary of the WCC expressed his shock, deplored the denial of basic human rights involved in this execution and appealed to the Ethiopian authorities "to ensure that those still in detention are given the benefit of fair trial, legal defense and public hearing in impartial tribunals".[4]

It was felt that there was no need to consult the churches about this statement. The information about the executions came from the government itself, and the extent of human rights violations in the country was evident. But the statement deliberately refrained from passing judgement on the political situation emerging in Ethiopia after the military coup: this was a matter on which a judgement could be made only after consultation with the churches.

During the 1983 WCC assembly in Vancouver, violent attacks on Tamils in Colombo, Sri Lanka, caused the death of hundreds and left thousands of others homeless. A telex message to the director of the CCIA, who was attending the assembly, with details of the incidents was sent through the WCC office in Geneva. This was actually information given to the WCC by the Tamil Information Centre in London. A copy of this message came into the possession of the Sri Lankan government, which took it as information published by the CCIA. The matter was discussed in the Sri Lankan cabinet, and the churches in Sri Lanka were asked to dissociate themselves from the "statement". It required considerable effort to convince the Sri Lankan government about the status of the telex message. This incident shows how delicate the handling of information is, as well as one of the reasons churches may be very sensitive about international publicity or information regarding their situation.

Many churches in the middle of a national crisis are either reluctant to be consulted or do not expect or want consultation at all. Or a church may maintain that it is up to the WCC to deal with these issues according to its own best judgement, and that there is no need to draw them into it. A critical issue is *when* a church would like developments within its nation to be internationalized. Churches will sometimes say, at least at certain stages in the development of a problem, that they would prefer to deal with it themselves and that there is no need for intervention from outside.

This raises a wider issue. While it is definitely within the purview of a church to recommend at a certain stage of a problem that it is preferable not to have international *action*, it should not say that there should be no international *concern*. Nor should it give cover to the familiar argument of governments that these are all "internal matters". International concern about human dignity and justice, anywhere in the world, is part of the mission of the church universal and is increasingly being recognized as a legitimate concern of the international community as well.

The WCC has sometimes taken actions contrary to the advice of member churches. In other situations, WCC actions have been criticized by member churches directly concerned. In such instances the WCC has acted taking into account factors including the possible strain in relations between the WCC and the churches concerned and the possible reaction of the government and its effect on the churches.

When the Indian government imposed emergency rule in the country in 1974, the WCC general secretary made an appeal to the Indian prime minister Indira Gandhi, especially expressing concern about the detention of thousands of political prisoners without trial. This appeal was made three months after the declaration of the emergency, during which time formal and informal consultations with the churches in India had given the impression that official church bodies at least were unwilling to take any critical stance vis-a-vis the government, although a few prominent church leaders had spoken out. Indeed, some church bodies had gone to the extent of supporting the emergency rule. The churches seemed unwilling to look at the larger picture of human rights violations and were apparently more concerned about what they perceived to be their own minority and institutional interests. Through the CCIA, the WCC tried to engage the Indian churches and the National Christian Council of India in a dialogue on the long-term implications of the governmental action, but there was little response. It is now generally recognized that the emergency rule substantially weakened democratic institutions and eroded democratic values in India.

In October 1983 the United States invaded the small Caribbean island state of Grenada. In trying to formulate a policy, the WCC sought to consult the churches in Grenada, which were in disarray at that time. The WCC joined the Caribbean Conference of Churches in deploring the invasion of Grenada.

It was apparent that some churches in Grenada were inclined to favour outside intervention in view of the trauma of the internal violence that had preceded the invasion. But the regional body and the WCC had to differ from this view. Seen from a regional and global perspective, the invasion of Grenada had several implications. To begin with, this was a flagrant violation of international law. It was creating an extremely dangerous precedent for military intervention with arguments and pretexts that could be used in other situations — this at a time when the USA was known to be actively considering military action against Nicaragua. The WCC felt that the invasion had to be condemned, recognizing that in such instances perceptions from a national perspective can differ from those from an international perspective. This is part of the creative tension in the fellowship of the churches.

The churches' reluctance may also stem from a genuine belief that international publicity will be counter-productive, that it may render national effort ineffective and may be even construed as anti-national propaganda. In such circumstances a church may feel that international action will harm its interests, at least in the short term. While such a position should be appreciated by the WCC, the judgement of the international body may be different. This often poses a genuine dilemma for the WCC, especially with regard to the timing of an action.

A case in point is that of Uganda during the regime of Idi Amin. Despite information of massive human rights violations there for several years, the WCC's first public statement on the situation came only in February 1977, when Anglican Archbishop Luwum was killed.

Noted African political scientist Ali A. Mazrui wrote a scathing criticism of how the ecumenical bodies — the All Africa Conference of Churches and the WCC — turned the Ugandan calamity into a "religious crusade":

> The same church organizations had been "discreetly silent" for six years while Amin tortured and butchered... other Ugandans, both Christian and Muslim. Yet it took the murder of a fellow churchman to arouse the conscience of organized Christianity. With all other professional groups, it might be understandable to sit back until a fellow professional is killed before being aroused, but with churches such a record is not good enough.[5]

This is a very serious criticism. In retrospect, one can explain what happened. But that would not fully answer the criticism. It was probably a mistake for the WCC not to have taken public action earlier.

From 1973 the WCC had been in regular consultation with the Church of Uganda on the situation in the country and what the WCC could do. Several WCC and AACC officials discussed the issue with Archbishop Luwum during the WCC assembly in Nairobi in 1975. Luwum said he would let them know when the WCC and AACC should act. Soon after the central committee meeting in August 1976, the WCC again took up the matter with the Church of Uganda. At the end of 1976, Luwum told the WCC and AACC that he was making a final attempt, along with other Christian and Muslim leaders, to meet with Amin about the situation in the country, and that he would contact the ecumenical bodies after that. It was on his way to the president's residence that the archbishop was killed.

Undeniably the media have a strong influence on the selection and prioritizing of issues on which the WCC acts because of their substantial influence on international public opinion. Of course, this selection and prioritizing by the media can be misleading and distorted. Because of the way in which the present international information order operates, the media are dominated by Western interests, so that reactions to an event even in a third-world country are often based on Western perceptions. Some sectors of international public opinion will be highly critical of these perceptions. In the midst of these conflicting reactions and perceptions, the WCC must select issues for its own action and accord them priority.

Another difficulty is posed by changing headlines. An event today eclipses yesterday's tragedy, even if its consequences are continuing and may be even more calamitous than what is now claiming the greatest media attention. As the contemporary Czech novelist Milan Kundera writes in *The Book of Laughter and Forgetting*:

> The bloody massacre in Bangladesh quickly covered the memory of the invasion of Czechoslovakia. The assassination of Allende drowned out the groan of Bangladesh. The war in the Sinai made people forget Allende. The Cambodian massacre made people forget Sinai, and so on and so forth until ultimately everyone let everything be forgotten.

In a world of competing, shifting and vanishing headlines, it is possible to maintain a sense of perspective and proportion only by way of proximity to the people affected by the events; and churches and related groups are a valuable resource for keeping up such close contacts.

Yet a body like the WCC is not immune from pressure. With its headquarters in Europe and with the superior access that churches and the public in Europe and North America have to the communications media, information and interpretation of events often tend to be Northern. If something happens in which Europe has an interest, pressure comes on the WCC to take action. If something happens in a part of the world remote from Europe, there may be little interest and no pressure.

The Spanish dictator General Franco once sentenced six young men to death at the very time when thousands of people were being massacred in East Timor by Indonesian troops. There was an outcry in Europe and much pressure on the WCC to say something about the events in Spain. There was no concern in the European press about what was happening in East Timor. One could suppose that most people in Europe did not know what the latter situation was all about — nor even where East Timor is. Even in Portugal the concern was all about Spain, rather than the mess it had left in its former colony.

Of course the accuracy of reports and information is extremely important with regard to action by the WCC. An illustration of this can be given with reference again to Uganda.

When the WCC executive committee met in August 1976, there was a strong demand for a statement on Uganda, based on a detailed and sensational report in the London *Observer* about rape and massacre by Ugandan soldiers on the campus of Makerere University. The report mentioned the precise place where the events took place (on Freedom Square in front of the main administration building), the number of casualties (at least 100 and perhaps as many as 800), and details of brutalities (mutilation of women students) and sexual assaults.

Because of earlier difficulties in assessing the reliability of news about Uganda, WCC staff tried to verify the information. But members of the committee from the region had no information except what they heard when they came to Geneva for the meeting. In the end, the staff advised that no action be taken on the basis of the newspaper report and the central committee later passed a resolution calling on the WCC general secretary, in collaboration with the AACC, to take appropriate action with regard to the situation in Uganda.

Ali Mazrui, himself a former professor at the university, was in Kenya when the story broke in the British newspapers. He made his own investigation and wrote later:

> I have checked out the story meticulously, receiving confidential information from about fifteen witnesses who were on the campus on that day. The witnesses were of six different nationalities ranging from Ugandan to West German. I am now completely satisfied that there was no "massacre" on the Makerere campus in the first week of August 1976. There was indeed an "invasion" of soldiers, seemingly invited by the university authorities themselves in the face of student unrest. The soldiers did get out of hand and started beating up students, kicking them, injuring them with rifle butts. But nobody was killed. And apparently no girls were raped, let alone mutilated. In short, there was no "massacre" in the sense of killings.[6]

Mazrui says the British journalist mainly responsible for the story probably sincerely believed it. But he himself had not been to Uganda in the five years since Amin took power; and his first story was written from Lusaka, Zambia, and the second from Dar-es-Salaam, Tanzania. Yet this erroneous account by a sincere but mistaken journalist captured the attention of much of the world press. No retraction or correction was ever published by the *Observer*.

Pastoral visits

Delegations and pastoral and team visits play an important part in the WCC's actions in international affairs. They manifest the presence of the international fellowship in critical situations. They affirm solidarity, express the concern of the international Christian community and share experiences; and the impressions and information gathered through such visits are shared with WCC governing bodies, member churches and sometimes with intergovernmental bodies and the governments concerned.

From the many examples of such visits, we may mention three illustrations from the early 1980s.

In the Republic of Korea, 1980 was a critical year. The massacre at Kwang-ju, the death sentence against Kim Dae-Jung and the imposition of martial law made the situation in South Korea volatile. In the midst of those tensions the Korean churches were witnessing with commendable boldness, and many Korean Christians were suffering for it.

A WCC delegation visited the country in January 1981. It assured the churches of the unwavering solidarity and prayerful support of Christians in all parts of the world. The Korean churches voiced their deep appreciation for the visit, which they saw as a significant witness and expression of solidarity from the ecumenical fellowship in a difficult situation.

The WCC executive committee, meeting in July 1982 at a time when Israeli forces were continuing their assault on Lebanon, recognized the gravity of the situation in the Middle East and sent a delegation to Lebanon as a visible expression of its concern for and commitment to the people and churches there. Following their visit to Lebanon, they reported to the WCC central committee, which was in session. The siege of West Beirut was still continuing when the delegation was there, and its members gave a graphic account of the horrors of the situation and "the intolerable physical and psychological pressures on a people waiting for a final devastating attack. West Beirut is a powder keg, they reported, which could explode with unimaginable suffering and loss of life."[7]

This report received wide publicity in the secular press, and several diplomats subsequently mentioned how much they valued the first-hand information it provided. But to the churches in Lebanon what was most significant was the pastoral dimension of the visit.

Another delegation visited Central America just prior to the meeting of the central committee in July 1985. The ecumenical team went to Costa Rica, El Salvador, Honduras and Nicaragua. They were particularly saddened to learn of increasing attacks on Christian communities and on programmes and social projects operated by the churches. On the basis of the delegation's moving testimony about the situation in these countries, the central committee sent a pastoral letter to the churches there. One paragraph in it offers a good summary of the objectives of all such visits:

> We shall seek ways to multiply our opportunities for first-hand information from you through individual and group visits as well as through written and recorded data. We shall attempt to devise more effective possibilities for you to participate in and contribute to the worldwide ecumenical fellowship. We promise to tell the truth about you, your churches and your ministry to our own people and if possible to others, including our governments.[8]

Human rights

An important area of concern for the WCC is human rights. Two basic principles undergird the Council's engagement in this area: the responsibility of each local, national and church body for human rights work in its own area, and international ecumenical solidarity.

The first principle not only recognizes that it is those who live in a given place who are best qualified to interpret and analyze their own experience and develop strategies to advance human rights in their own situation but also that human rights are nowhere perfectly assured and that a church's concern for what is happening abroad must be tempered by an honest realism about its responsibilities at home.

The second principle speaks of the churches' responsibility to support one another morally, materially and politically. Many churches live in situations so grave that they cannot cope on the strength of their own resources alone. However, help must be sought by those in need, not imposed from the outside. Furthermore, in an interdependent world, the causes of human rights violations are rarely limited to any given local situation but are linked with a variety of international structural dependencies.

Many churches still need to be convinced that human rights struggles are an integral part of Christian witness or that their primary responsibility for human rights is within their own countries. Transnational solidarity for human rights is important in pressing norms and standards on the international community and in expressing continuous concern for promotion and protection of human rights.

International organizations that support local struggles must be seen as participants in the defence of human rights. One form of this participation is in providing protection to human rights workers, who are increasingly under pressure. Such activists must often pay the price of engagement by loss of their own security, freedom or even life. Among them are many church-related persons, who are threatened by detention, torture, disappearance and death. Support for human rights workers has thus become an important component of the WCC's action in this area.

Understanding the nature of local struggles is important for deciding what form international supportive actions should take. While these local struggles may generally be described as against human rights violations, they are also struggles for justice in the wider sense, since many of the violations grow out of structures of injustice.

Support for human rights struggles is not always free from ambiguities. One recent dilemma is related to the proliferation of internal and ethnic conflicts in which struggles for self-determination are often perceived as secessionist. The problem is how an international organization can support actions against human rights violations without supporting the larger cause or appearing to identify with it. Another dilemma is raised by the use of force by some sectors of movements struggling for human rights. Support for actions for human rights in such situations has to be carefully conceived and interpreted; and any violations of human rights by these popular movements must also be criticized. The dilemmas related to support for human rights amidst armed conflict should not be under-estimated.

Usually it is churches and church-related action groups which receive WCC human rights support, though it may also go to action groups which have no relation to churches. Sometimes individual Christians are active in these groups. Their non-partisan character is significant, especially where there are severe restrictions on political parties or when mainstream political parties are more interested in electoral politics and may neglect human rights.

WCC actions of solidarity with or support for local human rights struggles are moral, political and material. A significant form of support is advocacy — concrete activities to promote human rights and defend victims of human rights violations. Support is also provided to enable monitoring of events, quick transmission of information and the development of instruments and mechanisms to respond to violations.

Mobilization of international support through campaigns and building up of public opinion is another form of WCC action in favour of human rights. Access is provided to the international human rights system. The WCC regularly shares information received from local and national groups with the UN Centre for Human Rights; and it brings representatives of churches, national councils of churches and related groups to Geneva to offer testimony at sessions of the UN Commission on Human Rights. As appropriate, these groups may also be put in contact with other international non-governmental organizations with whom the WCC works closely.

The WCC's work on human rights has expanded greatly in all parts of the world since the mid-1970s, usually in co-operation with regional ecumenical bodies. Special mention may however be made of the Human Rights Resource Office for Latin America (HRROLA). The office was created in 1975 when military coups and repressive regimes were overwhelming parts of Latin America. Churches and ecumenical groups there were involved in human rights work, but no regional ecumenical body had been formed through which the international ecumenical community could channel pastoral support and funding and which could provide political analysis and information about the region.

HRROLA filled this gap. Its mandate was to assist churches in Latin America in their work to defend human dignity, to express broad ecumenical moral support for them, to provide systematic information on human rights in the region and to encourage Latin American churches to share their own insights and experiences across national and regional borders. With HRROLA's help, churches in several Latin American countries played a key role in the defense and promotion of human rights and in the transition to democracy. In several instances HRROLA assisted in the protection of human rights workers, the release of political prisoners and even in the saving of lives.

By 1990 the political situation throughout Latin America had changed and the Latin American Council of Churches (CLAI) was fully operational. While there was no longer need for a separate WCC human rights office specifically for the region, an evaluation of HRROLA's work underscored its contribution to building the capacity of people to address human rights issues in their own situations and the "frontline" character of its political analyses, advocacy and pastoral care, which anticipated areas of human rights needs and led the way for others to follow.

Conflict situations: prophecy and reconciliation

The first involvement of the WCC in an internal or international conflict situation is usually in responding to the humanitarian needs it creates. Sometimes the churches are caught between two sides of a conflict, placing special demands on the WCC. There are conflicts in which not only the churches immediately affected but also the international fellowship itself must take sides and extend critical support to one of the parties.

As a body of churches called to witness for justice and peace, the WCC has a special responsibility for initiating and encouraging measures for peaceful resolution of conflicts, whether by direct mediation, by encouraging persons or organizations who are in a position to initiate negotiation and mediation, by providing a channel of communication between the opposing parties in a conflict or by information-gathering and interpretation through fact-finding missions.

Perhaps the WCC's most successful and best-known mediation effort was in relation to the conflict in the Sudan, resolved through negotiations culminating in the Addis Ababa agreement of 1972. Such successes are rare, even for secular and intergovernmental bodies, and when they do happen it is often as the result of a series of attempts.

Hizkias Assefa has enumerated several requisites for a successful mediator: impartiality regarding the issue in dispute, independence of all the parties to the conflict but respect of and accessibility to them, knowledge and skill to deal with the issues, international support for the mediation and leverage — the possibility to put pressure on one or both parties to accept a proposed settlement.[9]

Assefa points to several advantages the WCC and the All-Africa Conference of Churches had for mediating the Sudan conflict.[10] As non-political, non-governmental and transnational bodies, the WCC and AACC could interact with the rebel groups without prima facie conferring any implicit or explicit political recognition, sovereignty or legitimacy on them. Thus the Sudan government could accept their good offices without jeopardizing its international image vis-a-vis the rebels. Moreover, they were religious organizations. Assefa quotes then-CCIA director Leopoldo Niilus, one of the chief mediators, as saying "that in a conflict where religion is an important factor in the inter-communal life of the parties, the intermediaries were better off if they were considered as people of religion rather than politicians even if they were from a competing or different faith".

The WCC's image in Africa was enhanced by the Programme to Combat Racism and by its 1971 central committee resolution on unity and human rights in Africa. These identified it as an organization which truly had the interests of the African people at heart and was working towards the attainment of justice in a continent that had been exploited and oppressed for centuries. British journalist Colin Legum wrote:

> The WCC had played an important part in bringing about these talks [the Addis Ababa negotiations], a role facilitated by its recent controversial decision to give support to liberation movements in Southern Africa. This action gained the confidence of Nimeiri and the largely Christian leadership of the Anya Nya.[11]

Traditionally, the missionaries and Christian churches in southern Sudan had been identified with colonialism and as being staunchly opposed to the Muslim government in the north. It was thus refreshing and attractive to the Sudanese government that a Christian organization like the WCC rejected the missionaries' perspective on the conflict and offered its auspices for peacemaking with due sensitivity towards the government's concerns. The WCC and AACC repeatedly proved to the conflicting parties that they had no axe to grind except to attain a peace acceptable to both parties. Their ability to maintain their special relationship with both parties without compromising their own independence was a great asset, further strengthened by the WCC's record of humanitarian assistance and its ability to provide aid.

Another factor facilitating the success of the mediation was a study sponsored by the WCC on "The Sudan Conflict: Its History and Development", which could be viewed as a diagnosis of the conflict by an independent party. By demonstrating to both parties that the intermediaries were familiar with the nature and complexity of the issues at stake, the study enhanced their credibility and probably had a positive psychological effect on each of the parties by making it feel that its side of the issue was understood. It may also have given each the benefit of understanding its adversary's position as stated and viewed by an objective outsider whom they could trust.

Unfortunately, by 1982 the Addis Adaba agreement had collapsed, mainly because of the government's failure to implement it honestly, and the civil war started again. The problem was made more complex by the government's introduction of *sharia* (Islamic law) in 1983.

In 1984, shortly before Sudanese president Nimeiri was overthrown, and again in 1990, the Sudanese government formally asked the WCC to use its good offices for mediation of the conflict. But although the WCC did initiate some processes, a number of new factors had emerged; and the WCC's ability to mediate was curtailed by the rise of Islamic fundamentalism and the government's impression that the WCC was supporting the Sudan People's Liberation Movement (SPLM). The WCC had a new image when seen through the eyes of Islamic fundamentalism. The government appeared to expect the WCC to use its influence on the SPLM to stop fighting. Such influence was supposed to be there because the SPLM leadership was "Christian".

This impression that the WCC could influence the SPLM on a religious basis was not confined to the Sudan government. A West German diplomat approached the WCC to intercede to secure the release of a German national taken hostage by the SPLM. The diplomat said he made the approach because the SPLM was an organization of Christians and so the Council could influence them. While trying to dispel that notion, the WCC did contact the SPLM with an appeal for the release of the German national on humanitarian grounds.

Elsewhere in the Horn of Africa, it was again the WCC's image as an organization concerned about liberation and human dignity in Africa that led the Eritrean People's Liberation Front (EPLF) to approach the Council in 1982 to seek the good offices of a suitable mediator in its struggle for independence from Ethiopia. The outcome of this was that Tanzanian President Julius Nyerere initiated a process of discussions with the Ethiopian government and the EPLF, with the WCC facilitating communications among the parties involved. As part of this process, Salim A. Salim (then foreign minister of Tanzania and later secretary general of the Organization of African Unity) met Issayas Afwerki (now president of Eritrea) for the first time. Years later, the mutual respect gained at that time and Salim's appreciation of the Eritrean issue proved helpful in some delicate discussions. The Tanzanian mediation did not succeed for a number of reasons. When President Jimmy Carter initiated a fresh negotiating process on Eritrea at the end of the 1980s, it was the WCC that persuaded Nyerere to accept co-chairmanship of the forum.

The WCC's non-governmental and religious character has helped in other situations as well. In 1975 the Iraqi government invited the WCC to visit northern Iraq in the wake of allegations of human rights violations following a revolt by Kurdish people there. The WCC was the first international organization to visit the area. When the team asked Tariq Aziz (then Iraqi minister of information, later its foreign minister and deputy prime minister) why other international organizations had not been allowed to visit Kurdistan, he explained that inviting delegations from the UN High Commissioner for Refugees or the International Red Cross might convey the impression that the Kurdish issue was "international", which would raise questions of sovereignty that were not involved by inviting the WCC. Moreover, Aziz said that the Iraqi government took into account the fact that the WCC is a religious organization.

These are only a few of the cases in which the WCC has initiated steps for mediation and negotiation in conflict situations. The wealth of experience the WCC has gained in this area needs careful analysis in order to determine the best course of action with regard to conflicts. What are the types of conflicts in which WCC efforts for mediation can be successful? At what stage in a conflict can WCC efforts be most useful? What experience can the WCC draw from churches and other organizations in this respect? It is apparent that two of the most effective ways in which the WCC can contribute to the resolution of conflicts are fact-finding and facilitating communication between the parties.

As mentioned earlier, there are some conflicts in which the WCC must take sides on the basis of its commitment to justice. But the function of taking sides and that of mediating are not mutually exclusive. In some situations supportive action for the disadvantaged party can itself lead to a role as mediator. Intervention in the name of justice in one situation may qualify the WCC for mediation in other situations. Prophecy and reconciliation can go together.

Quiet diplomacy

While the WCC is usually judged through its public actions (and particularly its public statements, the subject of Chapter 7), it should not be forgotten that a great deal of behind-the-scenes activity goes on. Failure to recognize this will lead to distortions both about the issues the WCC deals with and the actions it takes. The problem of course is that forms of action other than public ones cannot be made known.

Behind-the-scenes activities include information-gathering, information-sharing, discussions with churches, diplomats, UN officials and governments, as well as formal and informal confidential representations to governments and intergovernmental bodies.

A crucial factor in determining whether public action is appropriate in a given situation is the role of international public opinion. A public action by a body like the WCC has an influence on public opinion both internationally and within the country concerned. If an action by the WCC is meant to influence a government, such public opinion can sometimes be unhelpful. All governments are sensitive to public opinion. But the sensitivity works in different ways. Some governments are so sensitive that they will inevitably react negatively to criticism from abroad, considering it to be part of a propaganda campaign against them. This may be due to ideological reasons. Or it may happen that events have created a siege mentality in the government so that action by a body like the WCC is automatically construed as hostile.

The role of the media is very important in this connection. During the cold war the socialist governments in Central and Eastern Europe considered any criticism of their policies as hostile Western propaganda. A public criticism by the WCC would have elicited only a negative reaction — and thus accomplished little. This is not to deny that the WCC has an obligation to place on record its position on such situations. Another factor related to the media is that in countries where they are under control of the government, reports of a WCC action regarding the country, if made at all, will be distorted.

Critics have often charged the WCC with imbalance in its actions on the Soviet Union and South Africa. While many statements were made on the situation in South Africa, the WCC was generally silent about the Soviet Union. Here the issue was not one of selectivity: both were important and both were carefully monitored and followed up by the WCC. Rather, the issue was one of methodology, and here the effect of the methodology and the role of the media and international public opinion played a key role.

Actions or representations made confidentially may later be made public either because of lack of response or because it is judged that publicity would be helpful. One such instance occurred with regard to the trial of Georgi Petrovic Vins, the well-known dissident leader of a Baptist group in the Soviet Union. Appeals for WCC action came from several sources in the USSR, including members of Vins's family. (The writers of some of these letters made them public before they even reached the WCC.) The WCC decided to make a confidential appeal to the Soviet authorities, and a message from the general secretary was sent on 14 November 1974, which contained requests to make available the text of the indictment, to allow a legal observer at the trial and to provide Vins with the legal defense he had asked for.

There was no reply. When the WCC officers met in January 1975, information was received that Vins's trial was imminent. There was criticism of the WCC in the media for keeping silent. The officers decided to make a public statement reiterating the points of the appeal made earlier by the general secretary, adding that "we have reason to believe on the basis of information received that the charges against Vins are made primarily because of his religious convictions and activities".[12]

In 1980 when a WCC delegation met with a member of the Provisional Military Administrative Council of Ethiopia, he advised the WCC not to make public statements but to make representations directly to the government. For several years WCC staff held regular meetings on this basis with Ethiopian ministers and made representations on human rights, development policies and the like. As a result of one such representation, Abuna Poulos, now patriarch of Ethiopia, was released from prison. He had been detained soon after being made a bishop and was a member of the WCC central committee.

Legitimate questions may be raised about "quiet diplomacy" when carried on by a body like the WCC. The constituency of the WCC is not aware of all the issues which are being dealt with and what kind of actions are being taken. Silence may give wrong signals to those involved. The inevitable lack of transparency may be misunderstood as an attempt to avoid accountability. Contrary to other processes of ecumenical decision-making, "quiet diplomacy" appears to be undemocratic. Since the full story is not known, a distorted picture of the WCC may result. While such criticisms are legitimate, the fact remains that "quiet diplomacy" may be more effective in many situations and thus should be pursued despite its disadvantages.

The United Nations system

Through the CCIA the WCC plays an active role in the United Nations system as a non-governmental organization with consultative status.

An early and well-known contribution was at the time of the drafting of the Universal Declaration of Human Rights. The first draft on religious freedom read as follows: "There shall be freedom of conscience and belief and of private and public worship." The expanded version of this article, as finally approved, can largely be attributed to O. Frederick Nolde, first director of the Commission of the Churches on International Affairs:

> Everyone has the right to freedom of thought, conscience and religion; this right includes freedom to change his religion or belief and freedom either alone or in community with others and in public to manifest his religion or belief in teaching, practice, worship and observance.

It was in the historical context after the second world war that the churches entered into a covenant relationship and formed the WCC, and one of the first tasks of the new Council was to assist in the healing of the wounds of the war. It was natural that the WCC would feel an affinity for the United Nations, established "to save succeeding generations from the scourge of war and to reaffirm faith in fundamental human rights, in the dignity and worth of the human person, in the equal rights of men and women and of nations large and small".

Within the UN system the WCC is one of the largest non-governmental organizations (NGOs); and the CCIA was one of the first NGOs accredited to the UN. But even before formal accreditation, it played a part along with other NGOs in the successful lobbying to include a provision in the UN charter (Article 71) for the participation of NGOs in the work of the UN. It was also one of the organizations which played a key role in the process that led to the establishment of the UN Commission on Human Rights.

The WCC has periodically reaffirmed its support for the UN and exhorted the churches to support it.

The Church and Society conference said in 1966:

> The UN is the best structure now available through which to pursue the goals of international peace and justice. Like all institutions it is not sacrosanct and many changes are necessary in its charter to meet the needs of the world today. Nevertheless we call upon the churches of the world to defend it against all attacks which would weaken or destroy it and seek out and advocate ways in which it can be transformed into an instrument fully capable of ensuring the peace and guaranteeing justice on a worldwide scale.[13]

The central committee in August 1985 welcomed the 40th anniversary of the UN "as an occasion for the world community to rededicate itself to the principles and purposes of the UN charter, and to reaffirm the centrality of the UN in the conduct of international relations".[14]

The United Nations charter was proclaimed in the name of "we the peoples". But in essence the UN is an intergovernmental body, with decision-making solely in the hands of governments of member states. The main rationale for non-governmental participation in the system is that such participation makes the organization closer to "we the peoples". The UN becomes more international by NGO presence. When the UN made arrangements for NGOs to have consultative status, it was assumed that these NGOs would be of "representative character and of recognized international standing, representing a substantial population and expressing the views of major sections of the population or of organized persons within the particular field of its competence, covering, where possible, a substantial number of countries in different regions of the world". The

WCC can legitimately claim that it fits this description more than most other NGOs.

The WCC (through the CCIA) is in consultative status with the Economic and Social Council of the UN (ECOSOC) and with all major specialized agencies. Forms of WCC involvement in the UN system include formal invitations and submissions to UN bodies; contacts with the UN secretariat, divisions and agencies; access to the UN system for churches, councils of churches and related bodies; participation in UN events; information and evidence given to some UN bodies; and dissemination of UN materials.

Many of the most significant contributions of NGOs, including the WCC, in the UN system have been in the field of human rights. According to Theo van Boven, a study of the preparatory work for the International Bill of Human Rights reveals that "NGOs did participate in the debates on the drafting of the texts, at least on the level of the Commission on Human Rights and its drafting group, but they were not entitled to formally move proposals in their own name".[15]

Non-governmental input has been very significant in human rights standard-setting in the UN system. It was NGOs who pushed for more detailed standards in the area of freedom of religion, which finally resulted in the adoption in 1981 of the Declaration on the Elimination of All Forms of Intolerance and of Discrimination Based on Religion or Belief.

Van Boven says that fifteen years of NGO publications, written and oral submissions and "a good lobbying strategy" pressed the UN Commission on Human Rights to recognize conscientious objection to military service as "the legitimate exercise of the right to freedom of thought, conscience and religion".[16] Similarly, he adds, NGOs have played and are still playing "an instrumental role in human rights standard-setting activities" in such areas as the abolition of torture, the rights of detainees and prisoners, the rights of the child and the rights of indigenous people.[17]

In all these areas the WCC has co-operated actively with other major international organizations.

Especially through the Programme to Combat Racism, the WCC has worked with the UN system to confront issues of racism in general and in Southern Africa in particular. It has jointly organized consultations on South Africa and Namibia with the UN and has carried out some activities for the UN within South Africa. The WCC's monitoring of the transition of Namibia to independence won the appreciation of the United Nations.

The UN system also provides the WCC opportunities for informal contacts with high UN officials and diplomats. These contacts are used to exchange information, make representations to the UN and governments and to inform them of the views of the WCC on particular issues.

When then-UN secretary-general Javier Perez de Cuellar received the statement of the WCC's sixth assembly on peace and justice, he wrote:

> I was personally struck by the citation in the Council's statement from the Prophet Isaiah that peace is the effect of righteousness. In a world of such disparate mores and competing ideologies, the question might be posed "who is to define righteousness?" One of the great achievements of the human mind, I think, is to have answered this question in connection with the relationship between states in the form of the United Nations charter... There is no doubt that if all these nations complied with its purposes and principles the effect would be lasting peace.[18]

NOTES

[1] *The Role of the World Council of Churches in International Affairs*, Geneva, WCC, 1986, p.14.

[2] *Ibid.*

[3] *Ibid*, p.8.

[4] *The Churches in International Affairs: Reports 1974-1978*, Geneva, WCC, 1979, p.112.

[5] Ali A. Mazrui, "Between Development and Decay: Anarchy, Tyranny and Progress under Idi Amin", *Third World Quarterly*, vol. II, no. 1, January 1980, p.50.

[6] *Ibid.*, p.46.

[7] *The Churches in International Affairs: Reports 1979-1982*, Geneva, WCC, 1983, p.152.

[8] *The Churches in International Affairs: Reports 1983-1986*, Geneva, WCC, 1987, p.130.

[9] Hizkias Assefa, *Mediation of Civil Wars*, Boulder, Colorado, and London, Westview, 1987, p.22.

[10] *Ibid.*, pp.164-69.

[11] Colin Legum, "Fighting Ends in Sudan after 17 Years War", in *The Times*, 26 February 1972.

[12] *The Churches in International Affairs: Reports 1974-1978*, p.186.

[13] *World Conference on Church and Society: Official Report*, Geneva, WCC, 1967, p.130.

[14] *The Churches in International Affairs: Reports 1983-1986*, p.63.

[15] Theo van Boven, "The Role of Non-governmental Organizations in International Human Rights Standard-Setting", *California Western International Law Journal*, vol. 20, no. 2, p.211.

[16] *Ibid.*, p.213.

[17] *Ibid.*

[18] *The Churches in International Affairs: Reports 1983-1986*, p.23.

7

Speaking: For Whom and To Whom?

No doubt people's opinions of an international organization are largely based on their reaction to its public pronouncements. This is not surprising since it is usually through these statements that the general public knows about the organization.

The WCC is no exception. Its public statements on international affairs often receive attention both within the churches and outside. But as we have seen, this can be misleading so far as judging the WCC's actions in international affairs overall is concerned. The statements which receive media attention are selected by the media according to their own criteria; and statements which the WCC considers more important or parts of statements which are crucial in terms of the WCC's views may go entirely unreported. Furthermore, public statements are only one form of action by the WCC, as we saw in the last chapter, and in many situations public statements or other public actions are not the most appropriate response.

The first assembly of the WCC in 1948 set forth a rationale for public statements:

> With respect to public pronouncements the Council regards it as an essential part of its responsibility to address its own constituent members as occasion may arise, on matters which might require united attention in the realm of thought or action. Further, important issues may arise which radically affect the church and society. While it is certainly undesirable that the Council should issue such pronouncements often and on many subjects, there will certainly be a clear obligation for the Council to speak out when vital issues concerning all churches and the whole world are at stake.[1]

Ronald Preston mentions several ways in which ecumenical statements are useful. Besides helping individual Christians in their own decision-making, such statements may provide links between Christians of different confessions or even between Christians and those of other faiths or none. The process of formulating statements dissolves the division between clergy and laity, since the experience of both is needed. Moreover, Preston says, statements can serve as a "stimulus to creating a bad conscience when the society and perhaps the church as a whole is complacent". Finally, they can help the church "to achieve some purchase over events and not lag behind them".[2]

According to the rules of the WCC, public statements on any situation or issue confronting the Council or its member churches may be made by the assembly, to which all member churches send delegates, or the central committee. Between the annual meetings of the central committee, the officers of the central committee or the general secretary may make statements provided that such statements are not contrary to the established policy of the Council. Under the general title "public statements", the WCC has published assessments of situations, appeals to member churches, representations and appeals to governments and intergovernmental bodies, pastoral letters, resolutions and minutes.

The question of authority

The authority of such statements is defined in the WCC Rules as follows:

> While such statements may have great significance and influence as the expression of the judgement or concern of so widely representative a Christian body, yet their authority will consist only in the weight which they carry by their own truth and wisdom, and the publishing of such statements shall not be held to imply that the World Council as such has, or can have, any constitutional authority over the constituent churches or right to speak for them.

The point that the World Council has no constitutional authority over its member churches reflects the nature of the WCC as a fellowship of churches and applies equally to all its activities. Since the WCC has no right to speak for its member churches, the authority of a WCC statement derives only from its own "truth and wisdom" and not from the fact that it is the WCC which has made it. Furthermore, a WCC statement may be very significant and influential because it expresses the judgement of so widely representative a Christian body.

This representative character of the Council may affect how people perceive its authority and sometimes leads to misconceptions, as Richard John Neuhaus has pointed out.

Neuhaus disputes the view of one commentator that the statements of the WCC and other ecumenical organizations such as national councils of churches "have nothing to do with what's really happening in the churches" and that "they no longer matter very much". The truth, he says, is more complex. One of the reasons that "they matter very much indeed" is that they "engage the energies of some of the most thoughtful and talented Christian leadership in the world today". But, Neuhaus goes on, "this is not to say that they represent all whom they sometimes claim to represent".[3]

He then cites a former WCC executive committee member who, in testimony to the UN Security Council in March 1976, described the WCC as a "fellowship of... Protestant, Anglican and Orthodox churches throughout the world, involving approximately 400 million Christians". Neuhaus characterizes this claim as "preposterous". In fact, there is nothing preposterous at all about saying that the Council is a representative body of churches whose membership totals about 400 million, and the WCC spokesperson did not claim that the views he was presenting to the Security Council were on their behalf.

But there is a problem here between the real authority of the Council in these matters and its perceived authority. The inference may be drawn in many quarters that the Council *is* speaking for the member churches, especially if it is introduced as a representative body of these churches. Yet the representative character of the WCC is real, despite the limitations on effectively representing the churches.

Neuhaus is correct in observing that the WCC's role is in no way comparable to that of the Pope in representing hundreds of millions of Roman Catholic Christians; and that most Roman Catholics at least know about the Pope and attribute some degree of authority to him, including when he speaks to the world on their behalf. He adds:

> Organizations characteristically reach beyond their grasp. But if the claims of the WCC are sometimes ludicrously out of touch with the organization's mandate from its member churches and with its actual influence, this does not mean that the WCC is unimportant. Hundreds of millions of Christians are involved — in the sense of being, knowingly or not, implicated in the pronouncements of the organization. That is, except for the Vatican, there is no other international association of Christians that can compete effectively with the WCC's claim to authority.[4]

The WCC and the Holy See

Comparisons are sometimes made between the role of the WCC and of the Vatican in international affairs and the question is raised why there is no collaboration between the WCC and the Holy See in these matters. It is helpful to look at some of the key differences between the two approaches.

WCC statements are products of a council in which many Christian confessions are represented. Papal encyclicals and declarations are produced by the leader of one church and his advisors. As we have mentioned, the only authority of WCC statements rests on their inherent truth or wisdom. Even if papal encyclicals and statements do not fall in the category of infallible teaching, they are understood as issued by the vicar of Christ, whose teaching authority is doctrinally established.

Commenting in 1971 on the authority of Vatican statements, Ronald Preston spoke of a trend in the Roman Catholic Church towards conciliarity and shared authority, not only coming from the Second Vatican Council but also in the worldwide debate about Pope Paul VI's encyclical *Humanae Vitae*, which dealt with birth control. Preston wrote that "perhaps it will be seen more clearly that in the end the influence of papal documents depends upon their cogency being generally evident to the people of God, and the extent to which they draw upon the life of that people has a direct relation to the cogency being recognized".[5] However, many observers would maintain that this trend has changed during the pontificate of John Paul II.

The chief obstacles to WCC collaboration with the Vatican in matters of international affairs are differences in the structures of the two and in their place within the international system. Unlike the WCC, which has no constitutional authority over its member churches, the Roman Catholic Church has a very clear hierarchical structure of authority, at the head of which is the pope. The Vatican has often appealed to this difference in nature to explain its reluctance to collaborate with the WCC on social and political issues — even on critical matters where there was an apparent identity of views and where common actions could have made significant impact.

There is also an important difference in status within the international arena, especially the UN system. As we have seen, the WCC is a non-governmental organization with consultative status through the Commission of the Churches on International Affairs with the United Nations Economic and Social Council. The Holy See is a non-member state. This concept may be a legal fiction, but it does provide access to the UN system in a way that is not available to the WCC. The Holy See acts as a state with a foreign service and diplomatic paraphernalia of considerable experience and expertise. This "ministry" is secretive, undemocratic and far less accountable than most foreign ministries and foreign services, which, unlike the Vatican, are usually subject to some parliamentary and public scrutiny.

The Holy See often gives the impression in the international system that it is speaking for the whole Christian church, a misconception that is reinforced by the style of its utterances, the claims of the bishop of Rome and the significance attached to them by the secular press.

It is interesting to note how the Holy See explains its role in the international system:

> International conferences and meetings... are frequently attended by representatives of the Holy See... As participants on an equal footing with those of the states, or more often as observers, these representatives demonstrate the concrete interest with which the Holy See follows the problems of the international community, or directly shares responsibilities for the discussions and efforts that are being made to solve these problems.
>
> Some people..., owing perhaps to insufficient knowledge of the terms of the problem, seem to confuse the Holy See with the Vatican City, and they attribute to the Vatican City State recognition as a sovereign body admitted to the concert of states. The best doctrine however — it could even be said the doctrine to which there is hardly an exception — is that which agrees in recognizing the attribution of sovereignty to the Holy See as the supreme organ of government of the Catholic church. A full member of the international community, on an equal footing with the states, the Holy See finds itself in a unique situation. Its sovereignty is spiritual in nature. Its authority — which is also spiritual and religious — extends over millions of persons scattered all over the world and belonging to the most different peoples and countries.
>
> Its real kingdom is the kingdom of conscience. This does not prevent the Holy See to exercise a real influence, not infrequently a considerable one, in the life of the international community also, but rather enables it to do so.[6]

The text concedes that "this applies in a certain way also to other forces operating in the sphere of the spirit and conscience" — and in this connection "very respectfully" mentions the WCC — but indicates that it is pre-eminently true of the Catholic Church and the Holy See.

Whether or not all the claims based on the legal fiction of the Holy See as a state are sustainable, it is clear that the expertise and information of the Vatican are unmatched: diplomats consider it as one of the best listening posts in the world. But the well-known Vatican analyst Peter Hebblethwaite points to another side of the picture:

> The Vatican diplomatic service has often been criticized: in 1969 Cardinal Leon Joseph Suenens said its representatives were "spies on the local chur-

ches". During the Allende regime in Chile, the nunciate was daubed with slogans proclaiming, "the church is the church of the poor". The main charge is that diplomatic considerations inhibit prophecy. More bluntly: it may seem diplomatically preferable to support the status quo by propping up an unjust regime, rather than listen to the local bishops who denounce it as tyrannical. This happened scandalously in the last days of Somoza in Nicaragua.[7]

A more recent instance relates to Haïti, where the Vatican appointed a new papal nuncio after the military overthrow of President Jean-Bertrand Aristide in 1991. The international community on the whole, including the UN, considered the new government illegitimate, but the Holy See gave the appearance of being the only "state" to recognize this illegal government.

Ecumenical consensus

Part of the considerable informal authority of WCC pronouncements is derived from the ecumenical consensus on which they are built. Through often difficult discussions with churches and in conferences, a consensus is forged on crucial questions like human rights, religious liberty, disarmament, nuclear weapons. This consensus then may become the basis of one or more public statements.

The WCC recognizes the importance of consensus on both the principles the churches define together and the concrete positions that follow from these principles. But if a consensus is simply the minimum agreement possible, the prophetic dimension will be curtailed. The position of the WCC cannot be that of lowest common denominator among the member churches. So it is important for the WCC to stick its neck out and even prepare new positions while trying to build consensus, maintaining all the while a keen awareness of the many different attitudes and convictions represented in the ecumenical constituency and of the realities of the political situation, so that the new proposals may have a chance of being adopted. But the increasing diversity within the fellowship of the Council — theologically, confessionally, regionally and politically — makes consensus-building more difficult today than in the early years of the WCC, when churches from the North Atlantic world were predominant.

Should church bodies state only general principles, or should they also articulate and defend specific policy options? A perusal of WCC statements shows that in practice the Council has opted for the latter, sometimes undergirding these by explicitly stating general principles as well.

Some will argue that what is important is consensus on general principles and theological foundations and that there will not be much consensus on specific proposals and actions in any case, so that the WCC ought to confine itself to the former. (Others would even challenge the claim of consensus on general principles and theological foundations.) On the question of how specific a body like the WCC ought to be, the debate raised by Paul Ramsey's book *Who Speaks for the Church?* remains relevant more than 25 years after its writing.

Ramsey cites W.A. Visser 't Hooft's defense of the right of church leaders to draw concrete conclusions and take public stands on controversial social and political issues, on the ground that "concern for the victims of injustice and conflict is a most spiritual matter"; and the church's province is "spiritual matters".[8]

Prior to the 1966 world conference on Church and Society in Geneva, Visser 't Hooft said an effort would be made there to reach concrete conclusions on the major social and international issues of the time. These conclusions would be more specific than the somewhat general statements found in the pastoral constitution on "The Church in the Modern World" by the Second Vatican Council, the WCC general secretary said. Amid all the critical situations with grave moral implications, Visser 't Hooft concluded that the churches have a duty "to become specific to the point of indicating in which direction the nation or the nations should go". Ramsey maintains that Visser 't Hooft actually meant specific "directives" since the Vatican Council had given "direction" and Visser 't Hooft himself had said that "we have no right to give only counsels of perfection to statesmen".[9]

Ramsey argues that, so far as the requirements of sound formation of national policy are concerned, a series of specific proposals by a group of church leaders is as abstract as a counsel of perfection from the same source. A church or ecumenical body will not have all the necessary data; that can be provided only by a large number of specialists on particular issues or situations, "like an entire state department". Therefore it is not easy for bodies like the WCC to gather a balanced set of particulars.

Ramsey cites objections raised by two theologians to this view. Ralph Potter wrote, "I take it that at some point, perhaps at the gateway of Auschwitz, the Christian should speak very specifically about the outrageous crimes of his government". Similarly, asked Thomas Derr, "Doesn't there come a point when the church simply has to say 'no' to a particular policy (e.g. the church in Nazi Germany), and doesn't this 'no' also frequently imply a particular 'yes' to a specific alternative policy?" Ramsey says this case is an exception which only proves the rule.[10]

While there are obvious pitfalls in the proliferation of detailed church and ecumenical proposals on international affairs, mere statements or generalities are not sufficient for a number of reasons.

Certainly enough information must be collected before detailed proposals are given, and it is true that churches and ecumenical bodies do not have an "entire state department" at their disposal. But as we have pointed out in Chapter 4, bodies like the WCC do have access to information — some of it unavailable from other sources — which allows informed analysis on which policy recommendations and prescriptions can be offered. Moreover, the reality of how governments themselves use information is important. It is not uncommon that a decision-maker in a government acts on the basis of very little information on a given subject, even when much more detailed information is available in some other quarters of the government.

Roger Shinn has argued that what Ramsey calls the "exceptions" are in fact not so uncommon:

> The American church has too often refused to deal specifically with the evils of slavery, race prejudice and military action. Throughout the fabric of our common life are specific evils to be condemned, wrongs to be righted, acts of mercy to be accomplished. It will not do for the church studious to replace the church militant.[11]

While agreeing on the need for restraint in making public policy pronouncements, Shinn believes that "in its long history the church has erred more often by acceptance of the status quo than by premature criticism. It has erred more often by a silence that meant a tacit support of the Establishment than by deeds of ethical daring."[12]

John C. Bennett agrees with Ramsey that "the greater part of what church bodies say should be in the middle area where theology and social ethics overlap", but contends that, "if this Christian perspective is emphasized in the light of the social realities, there should from time to time be more specific forms of teaching and action related to the concrete decisions of the government". He adds:

> If a Christian body never felt driven to relate its basic teaching to specific issues, this would be a sign that Christians were not very much concerned. Ramsey wants to wait until there is a position in the church that is beyond significant debate, but this would involve a strong inhibition against speaking at all about specific decisions. I think that a sounder position in the long run is

> more likely to come from a process that would include the risk of error in speaking than from Ramsey's inhibition against speaking.[13]

In various contexts the WCC has risked both the error of speaking and the error of silence. It has been criticized for speaking too often on some issues and keeping silent on some others. While some have said that ecumenical pronouncements are too vague and general to be useful, others have said they are too specific.

Middle axioms

A well-known but sometimes disputed ecumenical effort to reach a half-way house between generalities and details of policy is the appeal to "middle axioms". Broadly defined, these are statements indicating agreement by those from different experiences, working together on an issue, about the general direction in which Christian opinion should try to influence change, without going into the details of policy or the best way to bring it about.

The Oxford conference in 1937 spoke of the intermediate and interim nature of middle axioms. "Thou shalt love thy neighbour as thyself", an unassailable principle for Christians, gives little concrete direction for action in most circumstances. Middle axioms, by contrast, while at best provisional and never unchallengeable or valid without exception for all time, are indispensable as interim principles for any kind of common policy in this changing world in which God's will must be fulfilled.

J.H. Oldham put the point succinctly in a preparatory volume for the Oxford conference:

> Between purely general statements of the ethical demands of the gospel and the decisions that have to be made in concrete situations, there is need for what may be called middle axioms. It is these that give relevance and point to the Christian ethic. They are attempts to define the directions in which, in a particular state or society, Christian faith must express itself. They are not binding for all time, but are provisional definitions of the type of behaviour required of Christians at a given period in a given circumstance.[14]

According to Ronald Preston, middle axioms "can be arrived at only by inter-disciplinary work between theology, moral philosophy and various disciplines relevant to the area under investigation, and also by drawing upon relevant practical experience from among those involved in it".[15]

Preston criticizes the tendency he sees in some ecumenical quarters to dismiss middle axioms and efforts to develop a blueprint for an ideal political order in favour of calls for witness and solidarity. He calls this a mistaken alternative, since it is precisely the aim of the effort to arrive at middle axioms to clarify what should be done in implementing whatever general goals the church may wish to advance, whether witness, solidarity or something else.[16] He cites the remark by Konrad Raiser in his introduction to the report of a WCC consultation on political ethics:

> It is my personal conviction that the very early proposal of J.H. Oldham to work out "middle axioms" to intermediate criteria still has value today, and that, in fact, we have followed this direction in many other areas of ethical concern.[17]

Criteria for speaking

Reviewing the experience gained in ecumenical work in international affairs since 1948, the preparatory materials for the WCC's second assembly (Evanston 1954) identified some criteria for the selection of issues claiming attention from ecumenical agencies. They remain valid today:

1. Is the problem inherently urgent?
2. Is there a clear Christian concern about it?
3. Is there a substantial consensus of worldwide Christian opinion on the line to be followed?
4. Have those who have to handle the problem been able to acquire a real competence in it?
5. Is there a reasonable possibility that a contribution may be effective, or an overriding imperative for Christian witness?[18]

The study went on to list some fundamental questions which the churches must bear in mind.

1. What are the particular doctrines or aspects of the churches' faith which supply a basis for Christian approach and action?
2. In what ways is the churches' approach distinctive, and how much ground is shared with men of general good will?
3. What lessons can be drawn from the churches' attempts to deal with these questions?
4. What features in the life, witness and unity of the churches themselves render Christian action in the international field more difficult?
5. Do the churches possess the spiritual and material resources for such action, and can they be mobilized when needed?
6. Is there sufficient agreement on the principles of Christian action for any agency to act confidently in the name of the ecumenical fellowship?

7. What are the long-term international objectives for which the churches must strive, without prejudice, to work in disputes and the causes of dispute as they arise?
8. What are the notes of warning that the churches must sound?[19]

These questions, some of which have been raised earlier in this book, are a useful reminder when we consider the relevance of the WCC's public statements.

Over the years the criteria for the public statements of the WCC have evolved. In 1976 the central committee identified the following areas on which it is appropriate for the Council to speak:

- issues in which the WCC has direct involvement and longstanding commitment;
- emerging issues of international concern to which the churches' attention should be called;
- critical and developing political situations which need the judgement and spiritual and moral voice of the WCC;
- areas about which the member churches expect the WCC to speak;
- areas in which a policy and a mandate for the WCC secretariat should be set.[20]

This list is not exhaustive, and it provides general guidelines rather than hard and fast rules. "Sensitive to the special nature of a situation and taking into account other forms of action, the general secretary, the officers, the committees or the assembly will have to decide whether a statement is appropriate or not."[21]

If, as the rules say, the World Council of Churches is not speaking for the churches, what is it actually doing? On this question Bennett observes that "anyone who speaks 'for' the church will have little that is fresh to say on new issues". It is preferable, he says, "to plan for a variety of forms of speaking 'in' the church, which would also in many situations be speaking 'to' the church".[22]

Commenting on Bennett's remark, Neuhaus asks

> Is it really true that there are no personal or corporate voices speaking "for" the church, presenting a message that is "fresh" and relevant to "new issues"? The most common understanding of the Christian tradition and its ecclesial representation to the world would suggest that there are and must be such voices. The idea that the WCC is but a forum for myriad voices speaking in and to the churches is not unattractive, but there is certainly no consensus that this is the modest and limited role of the WCC. We have already mentioned

> the confusion about whether the WCC is to be representative or prophetic. In either case it presumably speaks "for" the church(es).[23]

M.M. Thomas links speaking by the church directly to its prophetic ministry:

> The capacity of the church to exercise its prophetic ministry in the revolutionary world in which we live depends upon the church renewing its prophetic being, that is, its being in Christ for every man and all mankind. This is the content of the Oxford 1937 slogan: Let the Church be the Church. And in this period of history, it finds expression through taking seriously the political context of all its concerns for the world... Christian ecumenism can become the foundation for a genuine humanism only as the churches are prepared at once to affirm the catholicity of the church and to accept the strains on it of a politics of catholicity as they become involved in preaching truth to power and exercise not merely the diakonia of charity but also of political justice; and above all as they seek to provide theological inspiration, ethical guidance and pastoral ministry to their lay members and groups speaking and acting in politics. In such a context, the question "who speaks for the church?" is irrelevant; severally and together all of us do.[24]

The audience

To whom are the WCC's public statements addressed? The answer varies. Some statements will have several addressees, others a single one. One part of a statement may be addressed to the churches, another part to a government or governments and yet another part to intergovernmental bodies. But all public statements in fact speak to more than those to whom they are specifically addressed. Sometimes the addressee may learn about the contents of a statement only through a media report. President Banda of Malawi is reported to have remarked once that he knew about an appeal from the WCC to halt the persecution of Jehovah's Witnesses by government agencies only from the BBC. The appeal, sent to him on 31 May 1976 by the WCC general secretary, was probably suppressed by loyal aides. But the Jehovah's Witnesses heard about the appeal; after all, it was meant for them.

Other instances can be cited. A cable was sent by the WCC general secretary to President Ferdinand Marcos of the Philippines on the fifth anniversary of martial law there in September 1977, appealing to him "to grant general and unconditional amnesty to all political prisoners and to restore human rights and fundamental freedoms of the people". There was no reply from the Philippines government, and, as in similar cases, it may well be that Marcos never saw the appeal. But a response did come from several political prisoners in Philippine jails who wrote to the WCC saying how much they appreciated the action.

Similarly, during the Indian emergency in 1975, the WCC general secretary made an appeal to the prime minister about human rights. Since it was sent through the Indian mission in Geneva, it must have reached the prime minister's office, which probably ignored it. Nevertheless, when the appeal was made public, it was a morale booster for many political prisoners and persons who had gone underground, as several of them acknowledged later.

So the audience is much wider than the addressees. As their name suggests, public statements, while they may have specific addressees, are for the public at large. The audience is all people of good will — the "justice constituency" as it has sometimes been called. And as the role played by the WCC in the international system is increasingly recognized in secular circles, its public statements are taken seriously by many of them.

Discernment is an important element of Christian obedience; and in the specific case of ecumenical public statements this includes the ability to differentiate between the times to speak and the times to keep silent. For the WCC the accumulated experience of the years has evolved a discipline of determining, case by case, the strategic centre of a problem and the form of action indicated.

> Therefore, it should be stressed that apparent silence on the part of the WCC does not necessarily mean lack of action. There may be certain situations where no action is deemed necessary or feasible and therefore silence maintained. But most often "silence" means either a non-public form of action — which may be made public later — or waiting for an appropriate time to take suitable action. Such "silence" can be explained in retrospect, and it appears that it may be useful to do so in some instances.[25]

Statements on specific situations are likely to invite criticism from governments whose policies may be attacked and others who support such policies. There may also be criticism from those who disagree about the intensity of the criticism or who feel that a different course of action or set of proposals was called for.

We must accept the reality that a WCC statement, based on its understanding of the biblical foundations, gospel values and the particular political situation, may not be acceptable to all Christians. As we have seen, there is a process of building a consensus in the WCC on larger issues like human rights, justice, peace and racism, which gives it the basis for making particular statements on these issues. But there can be honest disagreements and differences of opinion within the Christian community on such positions, especially when they identify a particular political course of action. It may be useful to mention three recent statements which occasioned debate and even controversy of this type.

One was the sixth assembly resolution on Afghanistan (Vancouver 1983). The main criticism of the resolution was that it did not condemn the Soviet military presence in Afghanistan.

The large-scale military intervention in Afghanistan by Soviet troops occurred around Christmas 1979. Since the WCC executive committee was to meet in a few weeks' time, action was deferred. In a statement on "Threats to Peace" the executive, which met in February 1980, was highly critical of the military action by the USSR in Afghanistan.

It was known at the time of the assembly that a draft agreement on Afghanistan existed, made possible through the initiative of the secretary general of the UN and his special representative. (The agreement was finally achieved in 1988.) The UN secretary general had said in June, two months before the assembly, that there was consensus on 95 per cent of the agreement. The point of disagreement was the timetable for the withdrawal of the Soviet forces. It was also known that opposition from the United States was preventing the secretary general from proceeding with the agreement, although within the US administration itself there were differences of opinion because Pakistan had indicated its agreement to the draft at the beginning of 1983.

The WCC wished to support the initiative of the UN secretary general, which was at a very critical stage. Therefore it was felt that it would not be helpful at that time to denounce any of the parties involved. It was also considered important that any assembly statement on Afghanistan should be adopted with the support of the delegates from the churches in the Soviet Union.

The assembly resolution actually summarized the main elements of the draft agreement proposed by the UN and affirmed support for its initiatives. The final agreement on Afghanistan consisted of these elements.[26]

The statement by the seventh assembly (Canberra 1991) on "The Gulf War, the Middle East and the Threat to World Peace" led to a great deal of debate.[27] At the time the air war had been raging for three weeks; the brief land war began shortly after the assembly ended.

The statement called "urgently and insistently on both Iraq and the coalition forces led by the United States to cease fire immediately and to work for a negotiated solution of the Iraq-Kuwait dispute within the context of the United Nations". It appealed to the government of Iraq "to signal its intention and offer guarantees that it will comply with [the UN] Security Council... by withdrawing completely and unconditionally from the territory of Kuwait immediately upon the cessation of hostilities".

Assembly debate centred on two major questions. One had to do with the sequence of the ceasefire and the Iraqi withdrawal from Kuwait. The vast majority of the delegates were clearly in favour of an immediate ceasefire as that was the only way to avert an imminent and catastrophic ground offensive by the coalition forces; and an amendment proposing that the ceasefire be conditional upon the withdrawal of Iraqi forces from Kuwait was defeated. In part, the amendment would have provided a justification for the allied forces' military action. It is worth noting that the discussion on this amendment by delegates from various parts of the world closely paralleled the international discussion going on at that time.

A second, more fundamental controversy related to Christian approaches to war. The draft statement presented by the assembly's public issues committee sought to give expression to the broad consensus in the assembly in opposition to this particular war. While not opposed to general debate about Christian approaches to war, the committee did not consider this particular statement to be the appropriate vehicle for further exploration of this classical — and complex — issue. Within the churches and in the WCC, this debate reflected three general attitudes: just war theory, pacifism and justification of or opposition to particular wars.

The draft reiterated the affirmation of the Vancouver assembly that the "the churches today are called to confess anew their faith, and to repent for the times when Christians have remained silent in the face of injustice or threats to peace. The biblical vision of peace with justice for all, of wholeness, of unity for all God's people is not one of several options for the followers of Christ. It is an imperative of our time." The public issues committee did not accept an amendment which asked for a total rejection of war on theological grounds. The amendment which then came from the floor read as follows:

> We call upon you [the churches] to give up any theological or moral justification of the use of military power, be it in war or through other forms of repressive security systems, and become public advocates of justice.

That wording was accepted by the assembly with little discussion, and it was only in the next assembly session that many delegates, appearing to realize its wider implications, voted to reconsider the decision and remove the amendment. But the issue raised by the amendment is critical for the WCC approach to questions on war and peace.

Over a period of several years at the end of the 1980s, WCC central committee action on Romania led to growing controversy, heightened by the dramatic events in that country at the end of 1989 when the communist regime of Nicolae Ceausescu was overthrown.

On the basis of a request from the executive committee to the general secretary to report on the Romanian situation to the central committee in Moscow (July 1989), the committee's action was to receive the report. A separate resolution, moved from the floor, to criticize the Romanian government was rejected.

The general secretary's report expressed concern about the human rights situation in Romania in general and the situation of the Hungarian minorities there in particular. It emphasized the need for international monitoring of the situation in Romania. The general secretary followed the advice of the churches in Romania not to be openly critical of the situation, because "what might be considered undue interference from outside may be detrimental to the interests of the churches".[28]

At its meeting in 1990 the central committee felt otherwise. It recognized that there are instances in which public pronouncements on situations may not be advisable. As the WCC's 1980 world mission conference stated, alluding to the situation in Afghanistan: "There is a need to express repentance about our inability to be more specific in particular cases. This reflects both the painful situation many people continue to find themselves in and the sensitivity we feel towards these where specific mention might be dangerous."

But the central committee in 1990 felt that the situation in Romania a year earlier had in fact called for public criticism by the WCC. The central committee thus passed a resolution expressing regret for "its mistaken judgement in failing to speak adequately about the situation at its meeting in Moscow in July 1989".[29]

NOTES

[1] *The First Assembly of the World Council of Churches*, London, SCM, 1949, p.128.

[2] Ronald H. Preston, "A Breakthrough in Ecumenical Social Ethics?", in *Technology and Social Justice*, Valley Forge, PA, Judson, 1971, pp.36-37.

[3] Richard John Neuhaus, "Toeing the Line at the Cutting Edge", *Worldview*, June 1977, p.14.

[4] *Ibid.*

[5] *Op. cit.*, p.32.

[6] *Paths to Peace: Documents of the Holy See to the United Nations*, New York, 1987, pp.xxvii-xxviii.

[7] Peter Hebblethwaite, *In the Vatican*, London, Oxford University Press, 1987, p.74.

[8] Quoted by Ramsey, *Who Speaks for the Church?*, Nashville, Abingdon, 1967, p.26.

[9] *Ibid.*, p.28.

[10] *Ibid.*, p.47.

[11] Roger Shinn, "Paul Ramsey's Challenge to Ecumenical Ethics", *Christianity and Crisis*, October 1967, p.243.

[12] *Ibid.*, p.245.

[13] John C. Bennett, "A Critique of Paul Ramsey", *ibid.*, p.247.

[14] W.A. Visser 't Hooft & J.H. Oldham, *The Church and Its Function in Society*, London, George Allen & Unwin, 1937, p.209.

[15] Ronald H. Preston, *Church and Society in the Late Twentieth Century*, London, SCM, 1983, p.147.

[16] *Ibid.*, p.142.

[17] Konrad Raiser, "Continuing an Old Discussion in a New Context", in *Perspectives on Political Ethics*, ed. Koson Srisang, Geneva, WCC, 1983, p.12.

[18] *Six Ecumenical Surveys: Preparatory Material for the Second Assembly of the WCC*, New York, Harper, 1954, p.45.

[19] *Ibid.*, pp.50-51.

[20] *The Role of the World Council of Churches in International Affairs*, Geneva, WCC, 1986, p.19.

[21] *Ibid.*

[22] Quoted by Neuhaus, *op. cit.*, p.17.

[23] *Ibid.*

[24] M.M. Thomas, *Towards a Theology of Contemporary Ecumenism*, Madras, CLS, and Geneva, WCC, 1978, p.174.

[25] *The Role of the WCC in International Affairs*, pp.19-20.

[26] *The Churches in International Affairs: Reports 1983-1986*, Geneva, WCC, 1987, p.105.

[27] For the text of the statement and a summary of the debate see Michael Kinnamon, ed., *Signs of the Spirit: Official Report, Seventh Assembly*, Geneva, WCC, 1991, pp.202-16.

[28] *The Churches in International Affairs: Reports 1987-1990*, Geneva, WCC, 1981, p.138.

[29] *Ibid.*, p.141.

8

A Politics of Hope

A WCC international affairs staff member once wrote that his most significant experience during nine years of wrestling daily with global crises and life-and-death issues like the arms race, militarism and human rights was a celebration of the eucharist.

> What was so noteworthy about a communion service held in a meeting room in the Hotel Righi Vaudois in Glion, Switzerland, that Friday afternoon? The answer lies in the hopes and prayers of millions of people over long and painful years. That single act of receiving the body and blood of Christ Jesus represented the culmination of a difficult process for which many people have suffered and died. It marked the beginning of a new era, a visible sign of a longed-for unity which has yet to be realized.
>
> For the first time in more than forty years Koreans from both parts of a bitterly divided peninsula were able to share the Lord's supper together.[1]

The meeting which included that service was part of a long process on the peace and reunification of Korea, undertaken by the WCC and several other partners but inspired and initiated by the Korean churches, guided by the biblical imperatives for unity and peace. They were convinced that in order to enhance human dignity in their country, it was essential to work for reunification, which was the aspiration of the Korean people. The governments of both North and South Korea had manipulated this aspiration, instilling fear and increasing suspicion. With the passage of time the walls of separation became ever thicker, preventing Koreans from public discussion of reunification and making it a criminal offence to have contacts with people from the other side.

That was the context in which the churches in South Korea asked the CCIA to take major responsibility for a process that would enable contacts between North and South. It was recognized that the Koreans themselves are the primary agents of reunification. The churches in South

Korea that were in the forefront for the struggle for democratization also took the lead in the struggle for reunification. This process came to be known as the Tozanso process, named after the site in Japan of an international consultation on peace and justice in northeast Asia in October 1984, which aimed at creating a forum in which Christians from North and South Korea could meet face to face and contribute towards peace and the reunification of the Korean peninsula.

The Tozanso consultation asked the WCC to explore the development of relationships with churches, Christian groups and others in North Korea through visits and other forms of contact and to facilitate opportunities for Christians from both North and South Korea to meet in dialogue.

The first visit by a WCC delegation to the Democratic People's Republic of Korea took place one year later in response to a joint invitation from the Committee for the Peaceful Reunification of the Fatherland and the central committee of the Korean Christians' Federation (KCF). This visit provided a chance for extensive discussions with the North Korean government and the KCF (after delicate negotiations with the South Korean government), which paved the way for the next significant step in the process: a seminar on the "biblical and theological foundations of Christian concern for peace". "Glion I", as the meeting was called, brought together for the first time representatives of churches from North and South. It was on this historic occasion that the eucharist service mentioned above took place.

Glion was also the site of the second direct encounter between North and South Korean Christians in 1988. Glion II declared the observance of 1995 as a jubilee year for unification to be a "decision of churches in both North and South".

In July 1989 the WCC central committee, meeting in Moscow with representatives from both North and South Korea present, adopted a major policy declaration on "Peace and the Reunification of Korea". The declaration — the first on the issue by an international organization — said:

> The Korean division is in microcosm a symbol of the division of the world. If this wound in the human community can be healed, there would emanate from Korea a hope for all humanity. We pray that the cross of the Korean people can lead to an Easter for us all.[2]

The reunification of Korea has yet to happen. Although the cold war has ended, this division which resulted from the cold war still continues.

Yet a few not insignificant things have been achieved by the Tozanso process. The isolation of the Christian community in North Korea, where the authorities until a few years ago did not even acknowledge the presence of a church, has been broken. Today there are church buildings in Pyongyang and the presence of Christians is affirmed. The contacts between the church representatives facilitated by the WCC have been the only people-to-people exchanges so far between the two states. These have manifested the unity of the church.

The Indian ambassador in North Korea said during my last visit to Pyongyang that the WCC has done things in that situation which neither the UN nor any government has been able to. The point is not to indulge in presumptuous boasting about the WCC, but to recognize in all humility that there are matters in international affairs that the UN and governments cannot do but the WCC can do.

The problem of evaluation

So was the Tozanso process a success story? Certainly it achieved some things. But for several reasons it is best to be extremely cautious in speaking of success or even effectiveness on this or for that matter anything else the WCC has attempted to do in international affairs.

An international non-governmental organization poses a greater problem of evaluation than a national political interest group because of the greater size and more heterogeneous nature of international society. On this international stage, decisions taken are the result of complicated processes. It is practically impossible to estimate correctly how much or how little each group participating in the general discussion has contributed.

For example, it is legitimate for the WCC to claim that its appeals have led to the release of a number of political prisoners. But it cannot claim that they have been released *solely* or even *mainly* on the basis of the WCC appeal. A government weighs a number of factors when it takes a decision regarding the release of political prisoners. Most of these considerations are domestic and national. However, it may take international pressure into account, including that from non-governmental organizations; and in this case a representation by the WCC might also be a factor. There may be instances in which the international public opinion which motivates a government to act in a certain way has been mobilized or strengthened by the WCC.

As mentioned earlier, governments are increasingly sensitive to international public opinion and pressure, though this sensitivity can work in various ways. Some governments are not generally influenced by outside bodies, particularly those which have no clearly defined electoral significance. Yet someone who can offer a fresh angle, new information or particular expertise can — with luck and the right contacts — feed an idea into the process at a particular time.

But who decides whether an action or policy is effective or successful? There is an evaluation that can be done from outside by analyzing the content, the responses, the outcomes. The real judgement, however, can be given only by the people and churches directly involved in the situations the WCC has sought to address. It is up to the churches and people in South Africa, Namibia, Korea, Lebanon, Armenia, Chile, East Germany — and many other places — to say whether WCC action has been useful or effective. It is their evaluation that matters, not that of critics who speak of the decline in the WCC's influence in international affairs just because they strongly disagree with the stance of the Council. It is from the judgement and experiences of these churches that the WCC must learn its lessons and make the necessary corrections.

In earlier chapters we have looked at why the WCC acts in international affairs. The demands made on it almost daily by the requirements of seeking to live out the gospel message are evident. The WCC is duty-bound to be in the struggles for greater human dignity and justice. In fulfilling that duty, that mandate, that vocation, the WCC need not and should not think of success. There will be results and consequences. Some of these will be unforeseen, even unpleasant, so evaluation of actions and policies is of course necessary.

Nor should we have illusions about what can be achieved in international affairs. Political solutions are relative. While some gains in justice and in peace may be made through the transformation of a political situation, the temptation to romanticize should be avoided even while celebrating the victory of the people. The struggle for justice and liberation is a continuing one and each system is under the judgement of God. The limits of politics should remain in the forefront of our consciousness.

Ronald Preston calls for a "hard-nosed utopianism" which recognizes the "politics of inperfection" but then goes on to seek creative change.

> There is no immanent law at work in history leading us to expect permanent social and moral gains. There will always be a struggle to maintain any that have been made. And solving one problem is likely to reveal a new one.
>
> Hope must not triumph over experience. But neither must it give in to a pessimism which says that there is no hope for a better social order... From the

> gospel we understand that God's graciousness is present everywhere and at all times... Christians do not live in an alien world where God's grace is not operative until they bring it. This is the basis for a Politics of Hope.[3]

Preston notes that hope is in short supply today. Few are as optimistic as they once were about the potentials of technology; and "political and economic aims have been cut down". Yet, he insists, there are possibilities of improving this "unfinished" world.

> Christian discipleship involves commitment to political action to improve its structures. There are indeterminate possibilities of improvement. No barriers have been laid down by God which set limits to what human beings can achieve if they are faithful, hopeful and loving.
>
> The final ground of a Politics of Hope is that what God has begun in Christ will be complete and that our labours in the realm of politics are not limited to maintenance work; on the contrary, our striving to improve it will not be in vain.[4]

That conviction lies behind the involvement of the World Council of Churches in international affairs. Rather than counting the costs or the profits according to secular calculations, it goes on because of the assurance that its striving will not be in vain.

Views from the outside

Nevertheless, it is interesting to look at some secular perceptions of the effect of WCC's actions. A case in point is the WCC's action about holding stock in companies directly involved in investment in South Africa. A cynical view was expressed by *The New York Times* of 23 January 1973:

> No impact on the stock market was observed after adoption of the Central Committee's resolution ordering the Finance Committee to sell WCC holdings. Nor did the actual sale of $1.5 million worth of stocks, as announced at an Executive Committee meeting in January 1973, cause a ripple in capitalist circles.

That was of course one way of looking at it. Others looked at the decision in a different way. Anthony Sampson in his book *Money Lenders* tells the story in some detail.

What many people saw as the economic miracle worked by apartheid was built on "taking away from the black South African his humanity and treating him not as a human being, but as an economic abstraction, a unit of production".[5] The WCC action was based on the conviction that "banking and all commercial life — and all of life itself — come under moral judgement, and that there is no place where we may go and hide and say that we have escaped the eye of God".[6]

Sampson writes:

> The World Council needed a focus for action, and they found their opportunity in July 1972, when some banking papers called the "Frankfurt Documents" were leaked to an American church group. The documents showed that 200 million dollars had been secretly lent to South Africa by the European-American Bank, a consortium operating in the United States which had close links with the South African diamond trade, owned by six major European banks. The World Council asked all six banks to assure them that they would make no further loans, but they all refused.
>
> The World Council then withdrew their funds from the six banks, and urged all churches do the same. In Britain a Methodist minister took up the campaign against the Midland, in which the Methodists held shares, and by April 1976 a formidable group of British shareholders, including the (Anglican) Church Commissioners, the Methodist Church and the Greater London Council sponsored a resolution asking the Midland to make no further loans to South Africa. In Holland a well-organized protest group boycotted the Amsterdam-Rotterdam bank, which at first doggedly refused any concession but then dramatically changed its policy and undertook to make no new loans. In America, the general campaign against banks was having some effect, and eight banks promised not to lend any more to South Africa. One of them (Maryland National) was boycotted by black community groups and the United Church of Christ, until it sent a delegation out to Africa; the bank then totally reversed its policy, and even divested itself of existing loans to South Africa.[7]

Darril Hudson points out another effect of publicity given to the WCC's divestment from firms dealing with South Africa: an article in *The Guardian* on the low wages paid by British firms in South Africa. Hudson suggests that this article "may have prompted the British government to publish guidelines for such firms, pointing out that there was no fixed minimum wage and that in any case, fringe benefits could be provided. A House of Commons sub-committee proposed an investigation into wages and conditions of employment in UK firms in South Africa."[8]

Sampson gives another illustration regarding the new enthusiasm about international aid in the early 1960s: "The UN General Assembly... adopted a historic resolution, based on the recommendation of the World Council of Churches, proposing that the rich countries should spend at least one per cent of their national income on grants and concessional loans to the third world."[9]

Occasionally the WCC gets credit for saying some of the most obvious things; it gets greater credit when it is the first international body to do so. That often provides leverage in turn for future actions.

The WCC was one of the first international organizations to say that the Palestinian issue was not simply a refugee problem — as the UN treated it for a long time. The central committee recognized in 1967 "that no lasting peace is possible without respecting the legitimate rights of the Palestinian and Jewish people presently living in the area" and expressed its belief that "in supporting the establishment of the State of Israel without protecting the rights of the Palestinians injustice has been done to Palestinian Arabs".

That the WCC was one of the first international organizations to champion the cause of the Palestinians added strength to the words of the CCIA director, at a 1982 UN meeting on International Solidarity with the Palestinian People, when he asked the Palestine Liberation Organization (PLO) whether the time had not come to make a declaration of intent to recognize Israel's right to exist as a state. Several diplomats praised the WCC for asking this publicly. Such a declaration was made by the PLO six years later, and mutual recognition by the PLO and the state of Israel took place in 1993.

The WCC was also one of the first international organizations to affirm that China's seat in the United Nations belonged legitimately to the People's Republic. That the WCC did not have a "two-China policy" proved to be of immense help in later discussions with the China Christian Council and officials of the People's Republic.

During a visit to Hanoi in early 1981 two WCC staff members had a long meeting with Vietnamese foreign minister Nguyen Co Thach, who was enthusiastic in his welcome to the WCC delegation. What the Vietnamese people and government would always remember about the WCC, he said, was an open letter from WCC general secretary Eugene Carson Blake in July 1972 to US President Nixon on the bombing of dikes in North Vietnam. The bombing, about which first-hand reports had been made by Agence France Presse and Swedish television, made a substantial impact on public opinion in the West when the WCC letter was published.

We referred earlier to the statement by the WCC general secretary about executions in Ethiopia in 1974, noting that the direct consequences of this appeal on the Ethiopian authorities are not known. But there was a subsequent appeal which the Ethiopian government could not have totally ignored. It came from the secretary general of the United Nations and the president of the UN general assembly and was along the lines of the WCC appeal. It was issued two days after the WCC appeal, and a UN representative delivered a copy of it to the WCC general secretary. Later we were told that the UN action was taken on the basis of the WCC appeal, since "Ethiopia is a Christian country; and the WCC knows best about the situation there and what to say". While the appeals did not stop all extra-judicial executions in Ethiopia, it is known that a second group of officials did not suffer the fate of the first.

As we have said, even though one may be able to cite instances in which the actions of the WCC have been considered successful or effective, that is not the main point. The WCC is involved in this area because it has to be. In contrast to dramatic successes by short-term movements dealing with clearly defined single issues, the style of the WCC should reflect perseverance in pursuing justice and peace rather than aim at spectacular achievements.

NOTES

[1] Erich Weingärtner, in *One World*, no. 120, November 1986, p.4.

[2] *Churches in International Affairs: Reports 1987-1990*, Geneva, WCC, 1991, p.102.

[3] Ronald H. Preston, *The Future of Christian Ethics*, London, SCM, 1987, pp.214-219.

[4] *Ibid.*

[5] *The World Council of Churches and Bank Loans to South Africa*, Geneva, WCC, 1977, p.7.

[6] *Ibid.*, p.43.

[7] Anthony Sampson, *The Money Lenders: The People and Politics of the Banking Crisis*, London, Hodder & Stoughton, 1988, pp.180-81.

[8] Darril Hudson, *The World Council of Churches in International Affairs*, London, Royal Institute of International Affairs, 1977, p.122.

[9] Sampson, *op cit.*, p.102.

9

The Church and the New International Disorder

Addressing a joint session of the US Congress after the end of the Gulf War, President Bush announced that the allied action which evicted Iraq from Kuwait had been a war which enabled the United Nations to "fulfil the historic vision of its founders. Now we can see a new world order coming into view... A world in which freedom and respect for human rights find a home among all nations."

From time to time it beomes fashionable for political leaders to indulge in the visionary rhetoric of a "new world order". Most recently, the end of the Gulf War seems to have been one of those moments when such hopes are kindled. The end of the cold war had provided an unprecedented opportunity.

Within less than three years, little was being heard about the new world order any longer. Instead, the prevailing world situation seems more aptly described in the title of a speech made by British foreign secretary Douglas Hurd at Chatham House, London, in January 1993: "The New Disorder".

Yet all agree that the old international order, familiar since the end of the second world war, is gone. In this concluding chapter we shall look at some of the new factors and new dimensions of old issues which foster widespread disorder in the world today and thus create new challenges for the church and the ecumenical movement as they seek to fulfil their role in international affairs.

The cold war

The history of the World Council of Churches coincided with the history of the cold war for its first four decades, and it was inevitable that the cold war made its impact on the ecumenical movement. A fellowship called to transcend the barriers of nations had to wrestle with issues that divided nations. It was not easy to bring and hold together churches from the East, West, South and North. The antagonism and suspicion among nations placed obstacles to the building and development of all international institutions.

The cold war was not a static phenomenon. It had its dynamics, and its reverberations were not confined to Europe and North America. As nations everywhere were affected by the cold war, so were churches; and the WCC had to take this seriously. The slowness of the integration of the churches from the East into the ecumenical fellowship, ceasing of participation by the churches from China, contrary East-West perceptions about conflicts and the arms race, persistent mutual suspicion, ideological struggles, divergent perspectives about justice and freedom — all these cold war realities complicated the WCC's efforts to witness in the realm of international relations.

Of equal or greater impact on the life of the WCC was the emergence of the third world, a world of rising expectations and revolutionary fervour, which did not want to identify with either superpower. With the rapid increase in the number of churches coming from these countries in the ecumenical fellowship, it was only natural that the WCC's agenda was substantially influenced by them; and their aspirations were bound to be reflected in the positions on international affairs taken by the WCC.

For decades two major regional issues with global significance were virtually permanent features on the agenda of the WCC: the Middle East and South Africa. It was in 1948, the year of the WCC's inauguration, that the state of Israel was established and the National Party came to power in South Africa and began to put in place its apartheid policy. The consequences of these events were bound to affect the WCC in many ways in the years to come. Both situations raised political and theological issues which the WCC had to deal with, and the shadows of the cold war extended to South Africa and the Middle East as well.

The global reach of the two superpowers and the tendency of each of them to interpret developments anywhere in the world in terms of its underlying antagonism to the other resulted in bipolarity coming to be held as the defining feature of the contemporary international system. In sum, international relations meant relations between the USA and the USSR. When these improved or worsened, it was felt all over the world. It appeared that all the important decisions for the whole world were taken in Washington or Moscow.

So long as the bipolar framework appeared to be durable, questions of security focused on the military aspects of the equilibrium. There was good reason to believe that fear of nuclear war was an important element of stability, at least in Europe. Both Washington and Moscow were determined to keep the logic of confrontation from leading to a catastrophic conclusion, which meant that the bipolar system depended as much on tacit co-operation and understanding as on pure antagonism. Stanley Hoffman writes:

> The cold war had certain rules of the game which were tacitly accepted by the two superpowers of the time. Ethically many of these rules were questionable. These rules were dependent both on ideological competition and in a way on mutual acceptance of spheres of influence. Significantly while both superpowers relied on nuclear deterrence for their security there was a taboo on the actual use of nuclear weapons, even though occasionally explicit threats were made. Nuclear deterrence is basically evil because of the continuing threat to inflict massive damage on one's enemy and the very credibility of deterrence depends on the willingness to carry out such a threat. Moreover the morality of spheres of influence was also always questionable.[1]

During the cold war self-interest prompted the superpowers to court or support many countries around the world. A poignant illustration is the Horn of Africa, where Somalia and Ethiopia were the darlings of one or the other superpower during the height of the cold war but totally discarded when it ended. Somalia was the ally of the Soviet Union until the revolution in Ethiopia. Ethiopia was at that time an ally of the USA. Then they switched sides, with Ethiopia receiving massive military assistance from the USSR and major US military bases being built in Somalia. The military aid policies of the cold war period continue to play a key role in the tragedy in this region, most painfully enacted in Somalia.

Bipolarity did not explain all international relations, and it was always challenged by the non-aligned states, but it was the lens through which powerful cold warriors perceived and judged the world. When British Prime Minister Harold Macmillan made his famous "Wind of Change" speech in South Africa in 1960, Africans heard it as a message of his acceptance of the end of Western colonialism. But for Macmillan himself the "great issue" of the second half of the twentieth century was "whether the uncommitted peoples of Africa will swing to the East or the West. The struggle is joined and it is a struggle for the minds of men."

In 1946 Vyacheslav Molotov, the Soviet foreign minister, declared that "one cannot decide now any serious problems of international relations without the Soviet Union". There in a nutshell is the hallmark of a "superpower" — its perceptions of its own self-interests must always be taken into account by everyone else. With the disintegration of the Soviet Union, only the United States can now make that claim.

The breakdown of the communist regimes in the USSR and throughout Eastern Europe has been one of the most dramatic events since the end of the second world war. Besides transforming East-West relations, it has also brought new dimensions in North-South relations.

It was the abortive coup in Moscow in August 1991 that led to the disintegration of the Soviet Union, but the cold war had in fact ended even before that. The dissolution of the Soviet system was the result of forces unleashed by Mikhail Gorbachev's policies of *glasnost* and *perestroika*, forces which he had hoped could be controlled and directed by a reformed Communist Party. These forces gathered their own momentum and direction and led to the historic transformation within the USSR and the whole of Eastern Europe.

But the unipolar model can offer only a partial explanation of the world situation. Unipolar hegemony cannot be maintained in the new economic financial-technological age. The USA remains a superpower in military terms, but it occupies a less-than-commanding role in international economy.

The end of bipolar superpower dominance has naturally released a number of new forces and made a number of actors on the global scene more prominent. Aware of this, the US has become more selective in its foreign policy, focusing more on interests that can be directly related to its needs than on the comprehensive cover expected from a global superpower and alliance leader. Its recent policies on Europe show this. But belief in its special mission persists. President Clinton has said he is convinced "that only the United States can play the leadership role that we ought to be playing, to try to stick up for the alleviation of human suffering, the continued march of democracy and human rights, and the continued growth of market economies". And while reducing United States armed forces, he is determined "to keep this country the strongest in the world".[2]

Integration and disintegration

An important feature of the emerging global situation is the contest between the forces of integration and those of fragmentation.

On the one hand, barriers that have historically separated nations and peoples in politics, economics, technology and culture are breaking down. Technology and economics have become truly transnational.

Advances in communication and information technology have destroyed many frontiers between nations, giving new strength to inter-governmental organizations and multilateral institutions. On the other hand, forces of disintegration within nations and states are gathering momentum. Large states whose continued existence has been taken for granted have broken into pieces. New demands for nationhood — and the revival of old demands — threaten many more states.

Europe is an obvious example, where one can see both forces at work. While the process of integration proceeds, albeit with difficulty, through the European Union, it is disintegration that is prominent in the European scene as a whole. Globally also it appears that the forces of disintegration are the stronger at the moment.

To some extent the disorder in the international scene is caused by ethnic conflicts. The ethnic group has probably become the predominant grassroots political unit in the world today. Donald Horovitz notes that

> In the last two decades ethnic conflict has become especially widespread. Ethnicity is at the centre of politics in country after country, a potent source of challenges to the cohesion of states and of international tension. Connections between Biafra, Bangladesh and Burundi, Beirut, Brussels and Belfast, were at first hesitantly made — isn't one "tribal", one "linguistic", another "religious"? — but that is true no longer. Ethnicity has fought and bled and burned its way into public and scholarly consciousness.[3]

Horovitz explains that shifts in the international environment lead to the emergence and remission of ethnicity. Ethnic allegiances are usually revived by the wartime experience or emerge again soon afterward. In their periodic re-emergence, ethnic sentiments have been supported by the widespread diffusion of the doctrine of national self-determination.[4] As happened at the end of the first and second world wars, ethnicity has re-emerged with new vigour at the end of the cold war.

Certain other worldwide ideological and institutional currents have also fuelled ethnic conflict. The spread of ideals and norms of equality has made ethnic subordination illegitimate and spurred ethnic groups everywhere to compare their own standing in society with that of other groups nearby. The state system provides the framework in which ethnic conflict occurs. Its main goals are control of a state and exemption from control by others.

These conflicts have challenged and in some cases already redrawn boundaries and borders that had assumed validity and even sanctity after the second world war. As Erskine Childers points out:

> Throughout the cold war period, ancient cultural, ethnic and linguistic groups remained trapped and largely dismembered within artificial frontiers that had been imposed among them... Frontiers had been erected between people of the same culture, language and historical governance who had never known such barriers. This giant phenomenon of peoples, cultures, and resources trapped within exogenous and economically irrational boundaries has been a devastating handicap to stable and liberal systems of governance and to socio-economic advancement among most of humankind.[5]

Childers notes that "seventy years of imperial boundaries evaporated within weeks after the collapse of the USSR, unleashing ancient ethnic and other tensions". The peoples of the Central Asian Republics, which were created only in the 1920s by the USSR, must now struggle to build political systems.

The redrawing of national boundaries has made the distinction between internal and international conflicts even more difficult. Internal conflicts used to become internationalized as a result of direct or indirect intervention by outside states. But when multinational states break up and the new nations are still in the process of being recognized by the international community, there is a real difficulty in distinguishing between internal and international conflicts. From the time the United Nations adopted the first resolution on Yugoslavia in September 1991 until it expelled Yugoslavia a year later, the world body acted on the assumption that it was dealing with an internal conflict, whereas the fact of the matter was that the old Yugoslavia had already ceased to exist by June 1991. The UN's difficulty was understandable, because as far as any intervention by the United Nations is concerned the distinction between internal and international conflict is a decisive one.

Politics and religion: the new nexus

A prominent feature on the international scene is the apparently growing influence of religion in the politics of ethnic and national identity. There are situations in which ethnicity or nationalism is coterminous with religion or confession. So when references are made to Armenians they are "Christians" and to Azerbaijanis they are "Muslims". In the former Yugoslavia, where genocide is given respectability by calling it ethnic cleansing, it is conveniently forgotten that the Muslims of Bosnia are Serbs.

This identification of nationalism with religion poses a challenge to secular polity in many states. Mark Juergensmeyer speaks of a "new cold war", which is "characterized not only by the rise of new economic forces, a crumbling of old empires and the discrediting of communism, but also by the resurgence of parochial identities based on ethnic and religious identities".[6] Some argue that this has happened because of the failure of secular nationalism. The Western models of nationhood — both democratic and socialist — are seen to have failed, and religion is seen hopefully as an alternative base for criticism and change.

Others have interpreted it in a slightly different way:

> As political ideology recedes with the collapse of communism, the politics of identity and community of religion, ethnicity and gender have begun to occupy the space vacated by political ideology. Directly and indirectly, religion, ethnicity and gender increasingly define what politics is about, from the standing of Muslim personal law and monuments in India to Muslim and Christian Serbs and Croats sharing sovereignty in Bosnia to the Clinton Administration's effort to appoint a government that "looks like America".[7]

It is not only secular nationalism that is under threat but also pluralist political systems and societies. This has also resulted in insecurity and frustration for minorities and denial of their democratic rights.

The political influence of Islam is often cited as evidence of a threatening religious revival with political consequences. But the assumption that there is a genuine religious renaissance with consequent political organization is not valid. It is true that political mobilization in many countries misuses religion and religious identity, but this is not confined to Islamic countries.

Yet there is a good deal of talk these days about "Islamic threat". Muslim fundamentalism is pictured as the new enemy. "For a Western world long accustomed to a global vision and foreign policy predicated upon superpower rivalry for global influence if not dominance," observes John Esposito, "it is all too tempting to identify another global ideological menace to fill the threat vacuum created by the demise of communism."[8] It is true that Islam today constitutes the most pervasive and powerful transnational force in the world. But it is political myopia to view the Muslim world and Islamic movements as a monolith and to see them solely in terms of extremism and terrorism, generalizing the violent actions of a few while ignoring the legitimate aspirations and policies of the many. A selective presentation and analysis of Islam and of events in the Muslim world has led to conclusions that are misleading and often alarmist.

Western secular presuppositions are a major obstacle to understanding Islamic politics by tending to reduce Islam to fundamentalism and fundamentalism to religious extremism. The many forces of contemporary Islamic revivalism are subsumed under the monolith of "Islamic fundamentalism", which is equated with the violence and fanaticism of mullah-led theocracies or small radical guerilla groups.

The nation-state

In the post-cold war period several questions have been raised about the future of the nation-state. Their role has been challenged by other actors on the scene and they have been affected by new notions about sovereignty, legitimacy and international recognition. Demographic, economic, environmental and technological changes, all transnational in nature, have serious implications for the future of the nation-state itself.

But the continued prominence of the governments of states as the major shapers of international structures has to be conceded:

> They are not the only international actors; they differ substantially in size and strength; many have very limited capacity; some are unstable and others have even disintegrated; each has to modify its behaviour according to circumstances and the reactions of other international actors...; and states often fail to address adequately issues which are of great importance for the world's future such as the environment. Yet for all their limitations they are the main building blocks of international structures.[9]

Paul Kennedy suggests, however, that the important "actors" in contemporary world affairs are global corporations. "In an age of twenty-four-hour-a-day currency trading or, for that matter, global warming, have national bodies such as cabinets or commerce departments much relevance?"[10]

These global changes call into question the very usefulness of the nation-state itself. The key autonomous actor in political and international affairs for the past few centuries appears to be the wrong sort of unit to handle the newer circumstances:

> For some problems, it is too large to operate effectively; for others it is too small. In consequence, there are pressures for a "relocation of authority" both upward and downward, creating structures that might respond better to today's and tomorrow's forces for change.[11]

Kenechi Ohmae goes further:

> The nation-state has become an unnatural, even dysfunctional unit for organizing human activity and managing economic endeavour in a borderless world. It represents no genuine shared community of economic interests. It defines no meaningful flows of economic activity. In fact, it overlooks the true

> linkages and synergies that exist among often disparate populations by combining important measures of human activity at the wrong level of analysis.[12]

The "relocation of authority" of which Kennedy speaks is related to a significant new discussion of sovereignty. Former UN secretary general Javier Perez de Cuellar, in his last report to the general assembly, took up this issue from the point of view of human rights:

> The case for not impinging on the sovereignty, territorial integrity and political independence of states is by itself indubitably strong. But it would only be weakened if it were to carry the implication that sovereignty, even in this day and age, includes the right of mass slaughter or of launching systematic campaigns of decimation or forced exodus of civilian populations in the name of controlling civil strife or insurrection.[13]

The South

Another feature of the new global situation is the weakening of the South. A number of factors have contributed to this. The end of the cold war has meant that the strategy of many third world countries to play off one superpower against the other for their own advantage is no longer effective. Moreover, during the cold war the Soviet Union and its allies — for whatever reasons — championed many third world causes and used their strength in international forums to espouse and garner support for them. That support is no longer there.

Third world countries have became more and more dependent on the West and on institutions controlled by the West, particularly the World Bank and the International Monetary Fund. Globalization has considerably affected their domestic economic policies, which are increasingly decided from outside. This economic dependence has reduced their political manoeuverability in the international arena at a time when the end of the cold war has challenged the *raison d'être* of nonalignment.

North-South relations will be of crucial significance in international affairs in the coming decade. The South has not yet been able to articulate a coherent position in the post-cold war period, while the North, keen to absorb parts of the third world in its economy, seems ready to leave the rest of it to its desperation.

A welcome feature of the emerging international scene is the increasing acceptance of the universality of human rights and the responsibility of the international community for human rights everywhere. Universality is inherent in human rights. As the secretary general of the UN reminded the World Human Rights Conference in Vienna in

June 1993, the UN Charter is categorical on this score: "Article 55 states that the United Nations shall promote 'universal respect for, and observance of, human rights and fundamental freedoms for all without distinction as to race, sex, language or religion'. The title of the 1948 Declaration — universal, not international — reinforces this perspective."[14]

However, debates during the conference itself showed that universality is accepted with reservations by several countries, which define human rights in religious, cultural, economic and social terms. The secretary general admitted that "while human rights represent a common objective for the members of the international community as a whole, while each member of that community recognizes itself in that issue, each culture has its own special way of framing the question".[15]

Some observers feel that the end of the cold war and the apparent consensus between East and West may ironically have undermined important dimensions in the international discourse on human rights. Broadly speaking, the three "generations" of human rights corresponded to three political visions: civil and political rights were associated with Western liberal democracies, social and economic rights with Eastern European socialist states and development rights with post-colonial developing countries. Despite its attempt to be comprehensive, the declaration from the Vienna conference gives disproportionate emphasis to civil and political rights and does not reflect adequately the evolution of human rights through the United Nations in the 1980s.

More significant is the widening of differences between the North and the South, in spite of the compromises at Vienna. The views of the South were already clearly expressed during a January 1992 meeting of the heads of states and governments of the Security Council. The Chinese prime minister, while conceding that "human rights and fundamental freedoms of mankind should be universally respected", stated that "the issue of human rights fell within the sovereignty of each country and should not be judged in disregard of its history and national conditions. It was neither appropriate nor workable to demand that all countries measure up to the human rights criteria or model of one or a small number of countries".[16]

The Indian Prime Minister took up the same argument:

> It is important to note that the content and nature of human rights were conditioned by the social, traditional and cultural forces that prevailed in different societies. While the endeavour of the UN was to gradually move towards creating uniform international norms for human rights, such norms

> should not be unilaterally defined and set up as absolute preconditions for interaction between societies in the political or economic spheres.[17]

These arguments were repeated again before and during the Vienna conference.

The United Nations: a new profile

The transformation in the position and profile of the United Nations is perhaps the most remarkable feature in the global scene. There is a renewed sense of energy, and expectations and hopes for the UN have never been so high. The big question is whether the UN will be able to sustain and fulfil them. The secretary general, conscious of the UN's vulnerability as well as its opportunity, has warned against an "excess of credibility".

With the end of the long years of deadlock on security issues due to the cold war, the Security Council, operating closer to the intention of the Charter than at any time in history, has been active in a number of trouble spots.

The UN Charter lays down the principles and structure for the organization. It reflects the fact that the UN is not a world government but an arena of sovereign states. There is an in-built tension between the Charter's respect for universal and individual rights and the claims of its member states.

Demands are growing for the reform of the United Nations. One of the most common — and pressing — is for the restructuring of the Security Council, whose present permanent membership reflects the power equation at the end of the second world war.

> The Security Council is absurdly anachronistic... Many of the UN's 183 members feel alienated by the Council, which since the end of the cold war has been dominated by the Western three (Russia has been preoccupied with domestic matters; China is not greatly concerned with faraway places). The Security Council, say its harshest critics, has become little more than an extra arm of western foreign policy.[18]

In a statement on 31 January 1992, adopted at the conclusion of the first meeting held by the Security Council at the level of heads of state and government, the secretary general was instructed to recommend ways of strengthening and making more efficient the UN's capacity for preventative diplomacy, peacemaking and peacekeeping.

The report given by the secretary general included two important new aspects. One is the concept of "peace-building action" to identify and support structures to strengthen and solidify peace in order to avoid a relapse into conflict. The second and more important is the proposal to have on a permanent basis under the Security Council armed forces to be deployed to maintain or restore international peace and security. The Security Council has not yet acted on this proposal.

In the recent past the UN has taken action in a number of situations that might be described as internal conflicts of member countries. Actions with regard to northern Iraq, the former Yugoslavia, Somalia and Cambodia, though of different character, have raised critical questions about the role of the international community in internal conflicts.

Recapturing the vision

"The Church and the International Disorder" was the title of the section on international affairs at the WCC's first assembly in 1948. Today we may speak of the church and the *new* international disorder. This is a time for the ecumenical movement to recapture the vision of its founders and boldly take new initiatives and redouble its efforts in international affairs. More than ever this dimension of the vocation of the ecumenical movement is of surpassing significance.

The tasks remain the same as those outlined by the 1967 Hague consultation which evaluated the first twenty years of CCIA. They apply both to the churches and their fellowship, with the emphasis falling on priestly intercession, prophetic judgement, the arousing of hope and conscience and pastoral care for humankind.

Preston says the prophetic task of the church today begins with its own life — "a prophetic criticism of the pretensions and ambiguities of individual and corporate expressions of the faith".[19] More broadly, it is to assess and evaluate the profound changes taking place today. On the basis of evaluation, support can be given, critique can be made and engagement can be faithful. God's word for discharging this task today is known by discernment, which is achieved by putting one's understanding of human life, drawn ultimately from the biblical witness to Jesus Christ, alongside a diagnosis of what is going on:

> Discernment involves the ability to grasp the issue of one's own day in a dimension of faith. It involves a judgement on the events of the day, the tendencies at work and the secondary consequences of possible action. We have the responsibility to weigh what is happening in the light of the criteria drawn from the gospel.[20]

Such a discernment of the new international situation is urgent. The rapidity of the changes and the dramas and traumas of transformation make analysis of the post-cold war period difficult. The ecumenical movement must be aware of how the "signs of the times" are being discerned by churches in different parts of the world and gather together those new insights.

The WCC's positions and actions on international affairs have been based on consensus on a broad range of issues. It has never been assumed that such consensus is permanent. A new consensus has to be built when new issues arise. The special difficulties of consensus-building in a time of flux like today must be taken into account. One important task for the fellowship of the churches is to rethink some of its ethical assumptions about international affairs.

As the well-known ecumenical theologian José Míguez Bonino has pointed out:

> Ethics makes the ecumenical movement ever aware of the world in which it operates, both in the sense of the reality from which it emerges and the influence it exerts and should exert on it. As we stand on the threshold of a new century, that reality is rapidly moving; the growing pauperization of the majority of the human population (both in third-world countries and in significant numbers in the "developed world") reaches a point where it verges on massive genocide, while the expansion of economic, scientific-technological and communication media endeavour to create a homogeneous world market from which the majority will be excluded. At the same time, the geopolitical and ideological frontiers of East and West which defined the world from the beginnings of the modern ecumenical movement are becoming fluid in a movement whose direction we cannot anticipate.
>
> Such a situation presents to ecumenical ethics a twofold task. On the one side, we have the question of priority and commitment: Will the Christian oikoumene be simply integrated in this "world market" as its religious legitimization and "accompanying music", or shall it make the poor of the land the object and subject of its reflection and action? On the other hand, will it engage in the rigorous analytical work that is necessary to mediate that fundamental option effectively and to help Christians and churches make the concrete decisions that correspond to it in their different circumstances and possibilities?[21]

The assumptions and rules of the game in international relations seem to be changing fast. New norms are emerging or are being imposed. Changes in the role of the UN, its expanding jurisdiction and the lack of criteria for some of its actions indicate this. Thus it is all the more important to give new impetus to ecumenical enquiry on political ethics and international ethos.

The collapse of the socialist governments of Eastern and Central Europe and the agonizing search for new political and economic models have generated a new worldwide ideological debate. The dashing of the hopes and aspirations linked to Marxist utopia cannot put an end to the quest for a more just society which upholds human dignity. A renewed understanding of socialism is bound to influence this quest.

From its beginnings ecumenical social thought has reacted against the ideological debate between capitalism and communism. In the light of the churches' experiences in socialist countries and taking into account the changes that have occurred, the WCC cannot avoid making a new effort to respond to these new ideological discussions as it deals with international affairs today.

A critical concept here is democracy. The idea that democracy is intrinsically intertwined with market economy has recently gained currency. But there is no guarantee in this understanding that the cardinal principles of genuine democracy — including people's participation and justice — will be ensured. The emphasis seems to be more on the form of democracy than on its substance. The churches have an important role to play in supporting genuine democratic transformation, both conceptually and practically.

The churches have to take seriously the situation created by the grave political weakening of the South. The non-aligned movement today has practically no voice. It appears that the time has come for the ecumenical movement to make an even greater effort to understand the new perspectives, problems and aspirations of the South and to assist in articulating these, thereby challenging the dominant ethos and discourse of international affairs in a seemingly unipolar world. The churches must carefully analyze the new dimensions of the North-South divide and speak up for the marginalized and oppressed.

Some new challenges

We conclude with a brief mention of three areas in which the changing global situation poses new challenges to ecumenical reflection and action in international affairs.

Church-state relations. A new ecumenical enquiry on church-state relations is needed, taking into account the evolution in both institutions. Part of such enquiry should focus on the secular state and the challenge posed to it by religious nationalism. The break-up of multi-national states and the creation of new states — but also the general challenges to the nation-state which we have mentioned earlier in this chapter — directly affect not only church-state relations but also ecumenical relations.

In several countries new attempts have been made to define — constitutionally or by other legislation — the relation between religion and state. Some countries have sought to give new descriptions of secularism. New issues of religious freedom have been raised in many countries.[22] The fellowship of churches should give special attention to these developments.

Nationalism. The identification of religion with nationalism, the misuse of religion for perceived nationalist purposes and the violence associated with this also threaten ecumenical relations and the integrity of the church. The central problem with this new manifestation of nationalism is that it ultimately judges or tolerates every religion on the basis of whether or not it is useful to the state. Such nationalism is a denial of the universalism of the Christian gospel to which the church must give continual witness.

> The need has never been greater, among both the old and the new nations, for the church to demonstrate to the world its universal character. Christian faith, it should always be remembered, is rooted in universalism. To link God and country too closely is inevitably to make an idol of the nation-state... No one nation is God's nation, rather all peoples and all nations are equally dear and equally close to God.[23]

The ecumenical movement has a responsibility in those situations in which religion, and especially the church, is misused for nationalist ambitions; and a new theological examination of the nation-state would be useful at this point.

Conflict. Among the conflicts raging in the world today, some are relatively new; others have been going on for quite some time. Several of them are especially violent, with gross violations of human dignity perpetrated regularly. Many churches live in situations of conflict.

On the basis of its experience, a body like the WCC must identify the types and levels of conflicts in which it can play a role for resolution. In a few it may be able itself to mediate; in others it may be able to find a suitable mediator. In many others it should be able to facilitate communications between the parties involved. More effort needs to be devoted to identifying peacemakers and peace groups which can act with and on behalf of the ecumenical fellowship.

The intransigence and persistence of conflicts are matters to be reckoned with. What is the task of the WCC in a conflict situation for which no apparent solution is evident? The fact is that persistent conflicts can be faced only by a matching persistence in efforts at peacemaking. The moment for a possible breakthrough may come suddenly; and to be able to grasp such a moment one must have been patient and persevering.

For the many churches which live in situations of conflict which seem to go on forever, new forms of pastoral ministry must be developed. The international fellowship of churches has to be sensitive to such situations.

In all areas of international affairs, the ecumenical movement must periodically evaluate its methodology and styles. It has to evolve new models of actions, engagement and response, taking into account the changes in the churches and the nations.

The aim of the Commission of the Churches on International Affairs has remained unchanged since it was established in 1946. It sums up briefly why the WCC is in the field of international affairs:

> to witness to the lordship of Christ over human beings and history by serving people in the field of international relations and promoting reconciliation and world community in accordance with the biblical testimony to the oneness of human beings by creation, to God's gracious and redemptive action in history, and to the assurance of the coming kingdom of God in Jesus Christ... This task necessitates engagement in immediate and concrete issues as well as the formulation of general Christian aims and purposes.

For the WCC, for other ecumenical organizations and for the churches, those words describe an abiding vocation which is as relevant and challenging today as ever.

NOTES

[1] Stanley Hoffman, *Ethics and the Rules of the Game Between the Superpowers: Right vs Might*, New York, Council on Foreign Relations, 1989, p.84.

[2] Anthony Hartley, "The Clinton Approach: Idealism with Prudence", *The World Today*, February 1993.

[3] Donald L. Horowitz, *Ethnic Groups in Conflict*, Berkeley, University of California Press, 1985, p.xi.

[4] *Ibid.*, p.4.

[5] Erskine Childers, "UN Mechanisms and Capacities for Intervention", in *The Challenge to Intervene: A New Role for the United Nations*, ed. Elizabeth Ferris, Uppsala, Life and Peace Institute, 1992, p.11.

[6] Mark Juergensmeyer, *The New Cold War*, Berkeley, University of California Press, 1993, p.1.

[7] Susanne Hoeber Rudolph & Lloyd I. Rudolph, "Modern Hatred", *The New Republic*, 22 March 1993, p.29.

[8] John L. Esposito, *The Islamic Threat*, London, Oxford University Press, 1992, p.4.

[9] James Barbar, "The Search for International Order and Justice", *The World Today*, Aug.-Sept. 1993, p.156.

[10] Paul Kennedy, *Preparing for the Twenty-first Century*, London, Harper-Collins, 1993, pp.122-23.

[11] *Ibid.*, p.131.

[12] Kenechi Ohmae, "The Rise of the Region State", *Foreign Affairs*, Spring 1993, p.78.

[13] *UN Docs*, GA/46/1, p.10.

[14] UN Press Release SG/SM/5012, 14 June 1993.

[15] *Ibid.*

[16] *UN Docs*, SC/5359, 31 January 1992.

[17] *Ibid.*

[18] *The Economist*, 12 June 1993, p.22.

[19] Ronald H. Preston, *Church and Society in the Late Twentieth Century*, London, SCM Press, 1983, p.103.

[20] *Ibid.*, p.104.

[21] José Miguez-Bonino, "Ethics", in *Dictionary of the Ecumenical Movement*, Geneva, WCC, 1991, p.368.

[22] See Ninan Koshy, *Religious Freedom in a Changing World*, Geneva, WCC, 1992, esp. ch.6, pp.57-72.

[23] James E. Wood, *Nationhood and the Kingdom*, Nashville, Broadman, 1977, p.100.